Choose on Purpose
for Twentysomethings

Choose on Purpose for Twentysomethings

Finding Work You Love,
Places to Grow,
People Who Care

Susan Berg, Ph.D.

Neff Mountain Productions
Doylestown, Pennsylvania

Choose on Purpose for Twentysomethings
©2009 Susan Berg
All Rights Reserved.

Published by:

Neff Mountain Productions
Doylestown, PA 18901
Phone: 215-348-5969
e-mail: susan.berg@ChooseOnPurpose.com
www.ChooseOnPurpose.com

Cover Design: Kathi Dunn, www.dunn-design.com
Editor: Alice Lawler, alicel89@verizon.net
Illustrations: Dunn+Associates, www.dunn-design.com
Interior design: Dorie McClelland, www.springbookdesign.com

Publisher's Cataloging-In-Publication Data
Berg, Susan (Susan R.)
   Choose on purpose for twentysomethings : finding work you love, places to grow, people who care / Susan Berg.
      p. : ill., maps ; cm.
   Includes bibliographical references and index.
   ISBN: 978-0-9822631-3-6
1. Vocational guidance. 2. Career development. 3. Young adults--Vocational guidance. 4. Young adults--Life skills guides. I. Title.
HF5381 .B374 2009
650.14   2009923545

LCCN: 2009923545

Printed in the United States of America
14 13 12 11 10 01 02 03 04 05

For my children, Kirstin and Erik.
They inspire me, laugh with me and teach me.

A note on pronouns:

Rather than muck up the conversation in the book with clunky he/she pronouns, whenever I'm talking about a third person I'll simply switch off between he and she.

It's a good reflection of the mix of people you'll want to be working with anyhow.

Hints on How to Use This Book

Make It Work for You

- Flip open the book and let whatever ideas appear at that moment help you

- Pick the parts that work for you and stick with them — even use sticky notes

- Don't make it a once and done thing — visit early and often for a pick-me-up

- Handwrite — the fluid movement of hand connecting to thoughts works magic

- Jump around — skim the *Contents—Detailed* (pages xii–xv) and *Directory of Activities* (pages xvi–xvii) to find the heading that matches

Pinpoint What You Need

Flying Start
The first three chapters — **Launch** — get you moving this week. Whether just beginning, or on the way, this gets you organized and connected.

Handle Networking Nerves
Does networking sound too much like *work?* Do Phase I — **Launch**, then skip to Chapter 6: *Reaching Out*. This will lighten the load.

Get Un-confused
Dive into Phase II — **Discovery**. Explore options and actions without the over-analysis that could bog you down.

Ready to Decide
Go directly to Phase III — **Docking**. Get some common-sense guidance — including trustworthy approaches for making decisions and help coping with pressure.

Signposts to Guide You

Activities

Action steps to get you moving towards your goal. Learn to use these three moves:

![egg] 1 Hatch creative ideas

![gear] 2 Put your mind and body in gear

![target] 3 Hit the target

Tips

Guidelines you can "turn on" to get back to basics, gain your footing, and steer through bumpy situations.

PAY ATTENTION
Gut instinct

What's your next move?

Pay Attention Notices

When you see this symbol, stop for a minute, shine a spotlight on yourself and look for what you need to pay attention to now! in order to move forward.

Strategies

Ways to grease the skids, get you on track, and adjust your mindset towards success — found in the *Resource Center*.

Coffee Cup

A reminder to pull up, take stock and go with the flow. Just like you do with a friend and a warm drink at your favorite coffee house.

Contents — Quick Scan

Contents — Detailed

Phase II: DISCOVERY   Seeing Possibilities   63

Phase III: DOCKING   Engaging the World   **137**

RESOURCE CENTER   Getting Things Done   **185**

Directory of Activities

Chapter 5: Shaping Your Futures

Chapter 6: Reaching Out

Chapter 7: Managing Yourself

Chapter 8: Choosing

In Gratitude

All good work comes as the result of a team effort. Many hands did indeed make this work light, and they came because I asked for help and they were willing. Colleagues and friends recommended some, and others I simply phoned and made a cold call to.

By my side from start to finish was family — Kirstin, my daughter, served as the ever encouraging, spot-on critic; Erik, my son, provided in-the-moment feedback to keep me straight; and Jim, my husband, contributed as partner, as fellow researcher, as supporter and as co-worker. This was indeed a whole brain team.

Speaking of whole brains, Alice Lawler, my steadfast, left-brain editor kept my right-brain creations organized and flowing. And she became a friend in the process. On the far right-brain side was graphic artist ED Hose, who guided me with her insights, patience and humor.

And the cold call that got me started was to Jim Horan, author of *The One Page Business Plan*. I love his work and decided to (cold) call him one day and ask for help. He has been there ever since, as mentor, asking me big questions, and helping with little details. In addition, authors Suzanne Zoglio and Claudine Wolk offered their experience, and friends Janis Long and Mary Brownsberger kept me afloat by listening.

There are some teachers who inspired me and influenced my work. They include: Barry Oshry, who taught me about power and potential; Ned Herrmann and Ann Herrmann-Nehdi, who opened the world of whole brain thinking to me; Sandra Janoff and Marv Weisbord, co-founders of the *Future Search Network*, who shared their knowledge of great meetings that change lives; and Pamela Curlee, who deepened my grasp of mind-body collaboration. I dearly prize these relationships.

And last, but not least, is the wonderful advisory network — a combination of all ages and backgrounds — who willingly give their time and their talent to provide feedback and energy to this project. You can read more about the fun we have at the back of the book or online at www.ChooseOnPurpose.com.

Your project will feed off this same kind of energy — it's catching once you start. My deepest gratitude embraces these people — and extends to you — for being willing to begin. This provides the spark that keeps me, and you, continuing to choose on purpose.

Susan Berg

Phase I: LAUNCH

Flying Start

Beginning

The beginning of anything new, especially when it challenges you, holds an odd combination of tension and excitement. Making choices that shape your future career and life can both enthuse you and exhaust you. Beginnings make you stop and think. Do you want this? Are you excited about this? And beginnings are no small thing, because they can change the course of your life.

You may see yourself as either focused by a sense of purpose, or still looking for how you can contribute to the world. This book will give you the tools to sharpen the focus and pursue the job and the lifestyle of your dreams. But you aren't exactly sure how to go about it. You've heard all kinds of stories — often about how such a thing as unique purpose doesn't exist, how you need to get your head out of the clouds, and you're, well, "dreaming" if you think you can make that happen.

We all have a dose of dreamer and doer inside us. You have a sense of which way you lean. Most likely your doer side got you to choose this book. But to make this work we'll have to tap both your dreamer self and your doer self. Together, we'll determine what's missing to link your dreams to your actions. Then we'll face any obstacles in the way and move past them.

Making Your Dreams into Reality

Despite the obstacles you see in your way, you can make the life you dream about happen. In fact, "dreaming" is part of the process. But you know that simply wishing it so doesn't create a new reality. Things happen because you DO something about them. Doing something is exactly what you will experience here. **This book is about bridging the dreams of your future with what to DO today to make them happen.** Landing the job and the life of your dreams doesn't appear through magic. It happens because you figure out what you want next and then take action to go after it.

With all the self-help books out there explaining how you can have what you want if you only believe in yourself, it's hard not to be skeptical, especially if your picture of the future is pretty blurry right now. I'm skeptical—and I do this for a living! Like many, I can be a little hard on myself. I tend to see the stuff that gets in the way first. But there's something freeing about seeing the obstacles. Once you see them, you can make a plan to get around them, if you know what you want.

The tricky part, though, is figuring out just what it is that *you want*. The self-help gurus say that if you focus on what you want you can make it come true. But since when is it so easy to know what you truly want? And if you don't know what you want, then it's impossible to begin a project to achieve it. It's no wonder so many people wander around trying things out, unable to put their talents into play, or getting no satisfaction from their work.

I'm going to fill in the blanks between "manifesting" what you want and finding a place to begin. I'll help you put enough pieces of the puzzle together to get you to the next best step in your life and career. That means getting you prepared to make a choice you can be happy with. It also means putting your practical side to work, and feeling great about taking the next step. It means getting you going in this *Launch*—your ***Flying Start***—phase. I want you to worry less about the long and far out future, and work with what's here and now.

How We Each Got Here. You are here because you have a desire to get clear and to get moving on your life and career. I'm here because as a seasoned, practiced person, I've been through what you're going through. I spend my work-life teaching people how to get out of the situation you're in right now. My experience has taken me from advising business executives to counseling engaged couples, and from teaching troubled teens to coaching college students. As a business advisor and team facilitator I've worked with my clients and in my community on many change projects over the last twenty years, knee deep in frustration and anticipation, as well as progress and pride.

Over the last few years my children have matured into successful, happy twentysomethings. As one graduated from college, one stepped into the army, and both made early career decisions, I found myself in the role of coach and mentor to them and their friends. As we talked, I drew on the skills and tools I have been using for years to help teams in corporations create satisfying workplaces and get successful results. Before long, I was talking to many young career starters with interests that ranged from meeting planning to medicine, from selling sports equipment to sound engineering.

As these conversations unfolded, I was amazed at how lost these young people felt, and how unprepared they were to ask the right questions, make choices, and especially take concrete actions that build into a satisfying result. Many were frozen, overwhelmed, or simply uninformed on how to start. At first, I admit I had some typical thoughts of a seasoned person. "Oh, they just need to buck up and get on with it." But the consultant in me wanted to understand more. Why were so many people stuck in the same ways?

I suppressed my desire to assume I had it all figured out and continued digging as a researcher. There are so many things about your generation that are so like your parents (I know you're surprised to hear this, and we'll talk about these similarities later). While I unearthed these similarities, I also observed key differences.

In fact: the world has changed a lot over the course of the twentieth to twenty-first centuries. In fact: while your generation is so much like your parents, it is, of course, so different. Different, not only because of how you were raised, but different because you need to make choices and respond to a world that has sped up, dropped its old boundaries, and currently connects at the touch of a button. Our access to resources and relationships creates opportunities, endless choices, and an element of risk. And there's the dilemma.

The epoch of the newest generation is becoming defined as a globalized world, dominated by mass communications, and long entries into adulthood. Jeffrey Arnett, in *Emerging Adulthood* states, "To be a young American today is to experience both the excitement and uncertainty, wide-open possibility and confusion, new freedom and new fears."

This means you need tools and playbooks fashioned to help you in this fast-changing and open-ended world. In fast times, you need to call on skills like balance, paying attention to stress, and pacing yourself. You need to be grounded in doing things that are practical and results-oriented.

> "Get ready to abandon the life you planned for the life you were meant to have."
> – *Joseph Campbell*

Yet you also need the freedom to dream and imagine what else is possible. And you need mentors and guides for your brain, your heart and your soul—to help you carve out your own path, and do what one of my favorite writers, Joseph Campbell, describes: "Get ready to abandon the life you planned for the life you were meant to have."

If you're going to forge a path that uses all your skills and talents, it will happen in steps. It's not so clear, in a world with so many choices, which step to take first. My role is to provide enough guidance to help you know what you want and make good choices. Your role is to take the first step, go exploring, and take ownership of the choice you make. Once you own it, you're ready to dock at the next port of your career and your life.

Getting Guidance from Inside and Out

There is a way to search for the life and career of your dreams. While it won't manifest itself from thin air, it will respond to your effort. I have a process that will guide you and get you running quickly, but won't dictate to you. I think it's important to keep the balance between guidance and freedom so you can apply the guidance in your own way. It helps to see how the paths of other people have unfolded. Here are the stories of two very different people and how they have balanced outside guidance with their internal barometers.

Several years ago my husband and I met Sam at a workshop on physical fitness and balancing your lifestyle. He was twenty-eight years old, had an undergrad degree from Harvard, and a law degree from Yale. Some pedigree, huh?

As we came to know him better, though, he was the saddest twenty-something we had ever met. Bright, with a legacy of both parents from Harvard, he was destined (doomed?) to follow. He never questioned, and after all, how bad could that life be? But his story revealed a long history of following in his father's footsteps — including a law degree and practicing for three years. Then one day he just up and quit. That was only three months before we met him in the workshop.

We encountered Sam at a very pivotal moment. He was now faced with a steep hill to climb. After all this time, he was finally beginning to figure out what he wanted. His first act was actually admitting what he *didn't* want. That's a big step for someone who appeared to be living the silver spoon life. It's no small feat to say no to that kind of pressure. The workshop became his first stop for guidance in making this huge life shift.

Sam was struggling to find a place to begin his life. When you're living someone else's life, beginning your own is especially challenging. That's why "Begin" is such a key, deliberate first step. It sounds obvious, to just begin by beginning, but what appears as obvious isn't always easy to do. A little outside, objective guidance always helps. When Sam showed up at the workshop, he sent out his call for help, and we were there to begin with him.

You may know a Sam in your life as well. It takes some of us a while, along with a few hard knocks, to figure out how to begin. Vulnerable though he was when we met him, there was no doubt in my mind he was going to make it, because just coming to that workshop meant he was taking action to start over. So beginning — by telling your story and stepping up, going beyond just saying so — is the first, and most important step of the process.

Dianne, the daughter of close family friends, was a very different story. She had so-so grades in high school, went to a medium-sized college, University of Hartford, and became a classic "late bloomer." She did well academically at college, and that's when things started picking up for her. She wasn't sure what she wanted to do, so she started out by temping for a while. She loved this, because it exposed her to lots of different kinds of work environments.

Then she worked for a year for a local city government, and got interested in pursuing graduate work in environmental management. Her good grades in college helped her land a spot studying at Johns Hopkins. After finishing her degree she was ready for a change and moved to Arizona. City government work had been fun, and now she had strong credentials to identify a niche for herself, so she continued in municipal work for several years as part of a larger city's environmental management program.

All along she had some ideas of what interested her, but she was happy to let things evolve and to learn as she went along. She picked people's brains, trusted and consulted with her parents, and experimented with different kinds of jobs. Most importantly, she never took a job that she wasn't interested in, and that she couldn't get herself psyched up to do on a daily basis. She believed that the most important thing is to choose something you love, so you can love what you do. That became her guide, her mantra.

Now in her mid thirties, she has moved back East and works as a consultant, helping medium-sized companies stay stable and find ways to grow. She loves the troubleshooting side of her work, skills she developed in her grad program and jobs working in cities. Most interestingly, for me, is the balance she managed to keep through all of this. She makes great money, loves what she does, and still finds time to golf and enjoy her family and friends. She never let the early obstacles, lack of a "high-powered" background, or other people's opinions get in her way or convince her that she wasn't as capable as, say, someone graduating from Harvard.

Dianne grew into her career through a long series of baby steps. She used family and mentors close to her to help keep her eye on doing what she loved. Sam, on the other hand, grew through jumps and jolts. He spent a lot of years on someone else's path. In many ways, he launched his life the day he quit his legal job. He *chose* to avoid the path to bitterness and chose purposeful action instead. Even though he jumped a big hurdle, he ended up on his feet, dedicating his skills to the non-profit sector. Today, he uses his own experience with decision making to counsel youth who are at a crossroads between purposeful and directionless pursuits.

The Phases of Shaping Your Future

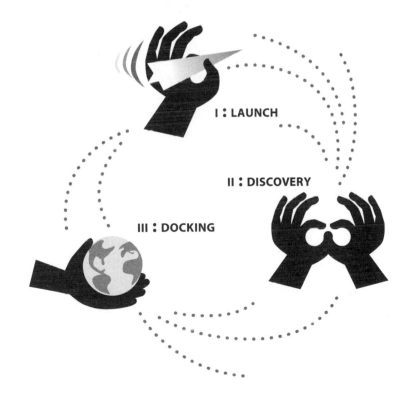

Whichever way the steps work best for you, you can see nonetheless that there are distinct phases in shaping your future. Sam's journey started once he figured out what he didn't want — that was his **_Launch_** phase. He ejected himself from one world and entered the second, what I call **_Discovery_**, like a deer in headlights — stunned by his confusion, but ready to move fast. Dianne, on the other hand, became something of a master at cycling through the _Launch_ and _Discovery_ phases. She saw every job, every opportunity as a chance to do more _discovery_. She's adopted an ability to work with whatever is in front of her. She never sees herself as done, she's always interested in who she meets, and what other opportunities might be out there for her.

Sam and Dianne's experiences speak volumes about the fine balance of guiding your life without locking yourself in to what others expect. Those "others" could be anyone — from family, to society stereotypes, to the voice in your head being too hard on yourself. In order to land in the next best place for you, exploring your needs, wants, skills and passions is paramount. While Sam and Dianne's paths to getting the next best jobs in their lives were very different, they are both well matched to their careers today because they paid attention to what they wanted and what they loved to do.

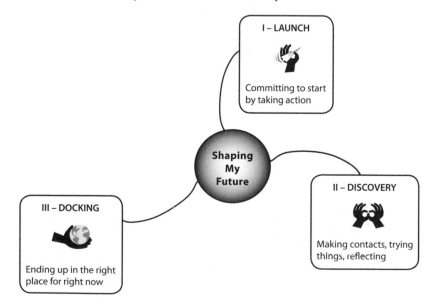

THREE PHASES OF SHAPING YOUR FUTURE

This leads us to the last step of this process — I call it **Docking**. By that I mean, ending up in the right place for right now. Life and times, needs and wants evolve, especially as you know more and more about yourself through experience. It includes awareness that you may need to unhook yourself at some point, to do some more discovery, and re-dock somewhere else.

Sam docked for quite a while in a place that someone else had picked, so it took time to face what he really wanted. And Dianne, while not focused like a guided missile, moved around a bit, enjoying the different experiences, learning how to dock and re-dock successfully. Both reached a point of getting to know what they wanted, but in different ways.

They were willing to be beginners, and to dock themselves at the next port that was ready for them, just when they were ready for it. It's a matching process. You really are a match for the world, holding a key that perfectly fits with some set of outcomes you are destined to create, like a key lining up with its catch.

The Elements of Your Journey

Regardless of where you start, this book offers the guidance to find what you want. Your journey may look a little like Dianne's or Sam's, or nothing like theirs. It all depends on your past, how much you pay attention to the choices you make, and how willing you are to look at all the factors that affect your happiness. I'll help you examine all of those elements. As you launch your search, you'll sift through the clues of your past, present and possible future. You'll also spend some time looking at how to manage three key questions that build your career and your life:

- What do you want to be?

- Where do you want to be?

- Who do you want to be with?

I'll help you learn how to pay attention to what's important, not just what's urgent, and how to make good choices based on the information you have in hand right now.

I am by your side, just as I am with every person I've ever advised. Your job is to participate in each step, even when it seems inconvenient or makes you feel self-conscious, edgy or sometimes just plain wiped out. All of these are signs that you're on to something important. Emotions may fly, from venting and complaining, to franticness and crying. I'll help you integrate these experiences into a new set of skills that will prepare you for a lifetime of transitions.

What You Can Expect. I am your guide. Since my family and I have had the incredible opportunity to work with a skilled glacier-climbing guide in the Canadian Rockies, let me compare it to that experience. Just like any good climbing guide will tell you, no two trips are the same. Even if you've hiked before, or job and career shifted before, this one is different, because you're different. You are walking into unfamiliar territory, and sometimes the mountain will be challenging to navigate. On a hike, these difficulties may appear as thin ice, rocks, or steep ascents. For you, the challenges will appear as confusion, stress, and fear.

As my family put our faith in our climbing guide, you can put your faith in me. The tools I offer you, like the glacier climber's tools, include steering, steadying, grabbing hold, and safe refuge. This guide will get you there, even in stormy weather and shifting terrain.

How It Works. I'm going to take you step by step through the three phases of the process—*Launch, Discovery* and *Docking*. I'll give you concrete things to do that get you started right away. I'll help you do enough personal exploration to assist you in the choice making process, enhance your sense of purpose, discover engaging activities in all parts of your life, and help you tell a meaningful story in interviews.

This is learning by doing at its best. I'll help you create experiences that move you forward, and I'll challenge you to be well rounded in all your thinking about the decisions you will make. And I won't let you squeak by without dealing with some of the messy stuff—like handling emotion, stress, frustration and confusion. They simply come with the package called change.

As you move your way through the book, you'll run into lots of discussion about important considerations for the change you're going through now. Sprinkled throughout the discussion you will also find *Tips* that have a proven track record, including tips on focusing in *Pay Attention Notices*. Most important are the *Activities* — the guts of what makes this work. Each one builds your experience and your skills to land your next opportunity. There's nothing tricky here—the key to the *Activities* is that they are active. They need your head, your emotions, and your physical attention.

Last but not least, you will find occasional references to the *Resource Center*. Here's where you can get more details, more explanation, and extra help for some of the things we will be working on.

Getting a Fix on Your Entry Point

It's time to put you on the field of play. Let's start by getting a fix on what you're moving towards. Change begins by figuring out not what you're running away from (that focuses too much on the negative), but rather what you're running towards. If you hate your current job or life situation, what is it you want to make happen instead? I want to get your head into moving ahead, and out of any bitterness towards your current situation. So here goes.

Tips Before You Start

1. It may help to set aside a particular time and/or place to do these activities.

2. It's easy to roll past this work and assume you know the answer. Pen to paper, however, always opens new vistas. Even if you roll your eyes occasionally at the things I ask you to do, persist anyway. Over the years, many participants in my workshops did just that, only to find themselves thanking me at the end for driving them towards action.

3. Don't try to do too many activities at one sitting, maybe a couple at a time — or you'll get bogged down and burned out. Pace yourself, and give yourself breaks. Starting fresh keeps your mind clear and your energy focused.

4. Consult Section 4 in the *Resource Center* on *Movement* to get more ideas on taking great breaks.

Activity 1

Moving Towards What You Want

GO

Write a letter to your current boss (don't worry, you're not going to send it), or if you don't have one now, a family member or friend. Tell them why you're leaving (whatever you've been doing) and what you're moving towards.

STEPS

1. **Dump quickly onto the page any negative thoughts you have** about where you are now and why it's not working for you. Describe what holds you back, how it's not the place for you to be and grow.

2. **Now write about what you want to make happen,** what you believe is out there waiting for you. Let go for a moment of your need to be practical, your doubt that such a thing could come true. Don't think about the effort it will take — even though I know that is hard to do. Suspend your judgmental, analytical, worrying side. Think about everything working out, for once. Describe what you are pulling towards, as if a giant magnet were drawing you to the next episode of your life. Write about all the skills, passion and knowledge you want to put to work.

NOTE: If writing to that friend or family identified above (not a boss), you may want to send it. It could help your friend better understand how to support you. Sending it isn't the point, though. You are documenting where you are, what you're moving away from, and where you are moving towards.

This is the beginning of focusing on what you want, rather than whining about what's not working. What you think about and how you talk about it really do determine what happens to you. The more you can shake loose of how crummy the market is, how nobody understands what you have to offer, your bad boss or whatever, the sooner you can begin discovering new opportunities. I wasn't kidding when I said the beginning step of the process is often the hardest. Part of beginning is being willing to let go of what hasn't worked, and look forward to what can.

Here's one more activity to keep shaking off the excuses and the distractions. This will take getting your body and your sense of humor in the game, so think about loosening up.

Activity 2

Shaking off Distractions

GO

Think of two or three things that are distracting you or bugging you and keeping you from concentrating on what you want to make happen in your life. *Now* you can open the floodgates and unload the key things that are getting in your way and preventing you from getting down to business.

STEPS

1. Write down key things that are in your way:

1)

2)

3)

2. Stand up and imagine they are all sitting on your left shoulder, like a giant bug. Walk around the room with them hanging on (or take a quick walk to the park). Remember, physical movement is part of the change. I'll explain shortly why this is so important. For now, just dive in.

3. **Grab what bugs you**, yell, "get off!" and rip it off your shoulder, throw it to the ground and stomp on it. Hard. Don't worry if you feel ridiculous — that's the point — finding ways to lighten the load.

4. **Smile. Laugh. Shake it off.** Walk it off and tell yourself how you won't be letting these distractions keep you from getting started on your discovery process.

NOTE: This is an adaptation from an old comedy routine by David Steinberg that we have never forgotten in our family. We sometimes ask each other "Hey, what's on that shoulder?!" as a reminder to let go of whatever is bugging us.

While I don't want to underestimate the things that can get in your way, start thinking about making this simple for yourself. Once you declare the path you're on and get busy working on it, it's amazing how things start falling into place. So let's start with what you have right now — capturing your current thoughts about areas of interest.

Starting Where You Are

Most everybody comes into this process with some inkling of what excites them and what they want to do. You may be thinking "Not me!" but I assure you, even if it's buried, there are some clues floating around and we're going to grab what's available. Let's start with even the vaguest notions. You'll have an opportunity to dive deeper in the *Discovery* phase, if that's what you need.

My approach for getting started evolved over coffee meetings at Starbucks and the like over the last couple of years. I've sipped many a latte with people looking for help getting started. I've found it works best if you get right at it by doing a quick and dirty download on what's flying around in your head.

As we begin the conversation over coffee, we talk about what fires you up when you think about making your next opportunity happen. What do you enjoy? What are your skills? Interests? Expertise? Start thinking about things you've done — work, hobby, watching someone else do something interesting — that have struck you as work you see yourself doing, that feels fun to you and powerful.

Let's tap into that right now. I've come to call this the **Coffee House Blueprint** — it's meant to be a working document, so don't be afraid to spill your thoughts along with a little coffee. Maybe you can work on it at your local coffee shop to pick up some of the conversational ambience. Go to the coffee shop (or your kitchen table) with a friend so you can bat around ideas about people you know, areas that interest you, and chat about this.

Activity 3

The Coffee House Blueprint (Spill Your Thoughts)

GO

Imagine yourself meeting up with me in a coffee shop. I'm the person sitting against the wall, medium height and build, chin length brown hair, black turtleneck, jeans, sipping a latte, and I'll have a yellow note pad open — looking around for you.

We start chatting, getting to know each other a bit. Then we turn our attention to a sheet of yellow legal paper. I turn it long-ways and draw three columns on it. Then I ask you to name three things you'd like to do. These things could be types of work, job titles, industries — or any combination of these. Don't restrict yourself — just think about what kind of work you'd love to do.

Next, you'll work your way through the steps outlined below. I suggest you draw it out on your own sheet of yellow paper. Make it your first working document that you want at your fingertips. The first three steps below match the three numbered activities on the sheet that follows these instructions.

1. **Work your way quickly** across the page and identify three areas of work that sound meaningful. Write it down without worrying about exact terms — remember, this is about tapping into what you know right now.

   If you're having trouble picturing a job area, check the *Resource Center* under *Picture Work You Love*. But, please, only do that if you are really struggling. I believe you have seen or experienced a taste of what you want to do somewhere in your life. Draw on that real experience.

2. **Write a few words** about why this sounds like an interesting match for you right now under each idea. Don't linger too long over this.

3. **Write down names** of people you know who are familiar with this area — this could be someone who does the job, knows people who do it, or works in similar areas. Among those names, identify someone in your family or among family friends that you would feel comfortable talking to now.

   If you can't think of anyone, make a note to talk to your parents or other close family members or friends to find someone. For this person (and others you may think of) jot down notes and contact information for people you might be able to meet with.

4. **Describe how you're feeling** and what you're thinking as you complete this. Jot down a summary of what you talked about with your coffee shop friend below. If you're frustrated, say so and either get help from a friend who can be supportive and encouraging (not someone else who will bemoan with you how tough it is) or go to the *Resource Center* at *Frustration 101*.

   This activity is important — I have personally seen it reveal Ideas that become a future job, a true calling. And clues show up here that can become important parts of your life in other ways — hobbies and pastimes that provide both recreation and contribution to the community. *Avoid the temptation to fret and stew — or worse — to skip this!* Get something down here. Then keep moving. If you're psyched — great! Move on . . .

5. **This step 5 may look small — but it is a BIG DEAL.** This is your moment to declare to someone (and the world) that you are searching for a new opportunity in your life. Now you have something to show this person when you talk to him.

   Use this *Coffee House Blueprint* to describe what you have started and explain that you are taking action. Choose someone who will be supportive — a parent, brother or sister, close family member or friend, including your friend from the coffee shop.

6. **This *Blueprint* is as good as your ability to take it "on the road"** — that is, to start networking with it. As you finish this activity I want you to start thinking about who you can talk to. In the next activity I'll help you get that started.

Bring It In. You've arrived at the middle of the beginning. You have now officially begun. You have put the thoughts down that have been rattling around in your head. Now that you have them identified, you can do something with them. You've had a chance at the "coffee house" — whether actual or in your own kitchen — to talk some things out with a friend.

Heads Up. Next, you'll sort out how to start connecting, networking and building a plan you can stick to. Remember, this works by taking small steps, and keeping active — you want to keep up your momentum.

The Coffee House Blueprint
A Design of Future Possibilities

	One	Two	Three

1. Name Three Job Areas:

2. State Why They're Meaningful

3. Identify People You Know
(possible connections)

4. What's on your mind
as you complete this?

5. Share your results with
a second person after your
"coffee shop" work session & chat.

6. Next step: Prepare to seek out others who may be able to help you with contacts.

2

Organizing

Organizing is so empowering—it tells you what to do next, and it can give you the satisfaction of crossing something off your list. Progress made. This chapter will take you through three important parts of organizing yourself.

First, we'll get your tool kit assembled. Since this is a combination of a personal remodeling project, as well as a climbing adventure, what you pack serves both your safety and your efficiency. This is where we'll make sure you have a serviceable resume and cover letter. The second item is finding a mentor—someone who can help you through this, from feedback to a shoulder to lean on. Lastly, I'll help you pull your plan together—this includes a plan to shape your future and a way to organize your contacts and your actions.

Tool Kit for Choosing on Purpose

Every remodeling project requires a tool kit. In order for you to be prepared and at your best, all your tools for the search should be at your fingertips. It helps to have an identified workspace as well, even if it's the kitchen table.

What are the tools for shaping your future? Like a carpenter, you need items that help you make rough cuts, and ones that help you finely shape the outcome you want to produce (see tool kit checklist on the next page).

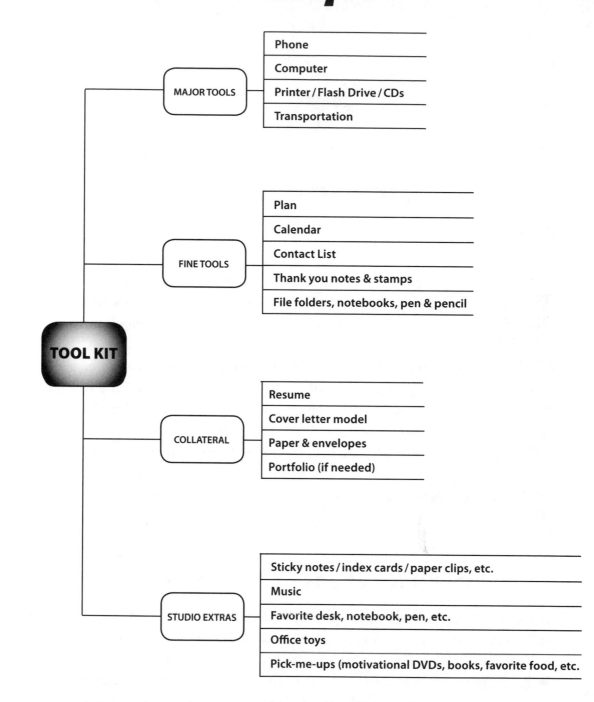

MAJOR TOOLS
- Phone
- Computer
- Printer / Flash Drive / CDs
- Transportation

FINE TOOLS
- Plan
- Calendar
- Contact List
- Thank you notes & stamps
- File folders, notebooks, pen & pencil

TOOL KIT

COLLATERAL
- Resume
- Cover letter model
- Paper & envelopes
- Portfolio (if needed)

STUDIO EXTRAS
- Sticky notes / index cards / paper clips, etc.
- Music
- Favorite desk, notebook, pen, etc.
- Office toys
- Pick-me-ups (motivational DVDs, books, favorite food, etc.

The **Major Tools** allow you to communicate with and access the people you need to connect with, whether in person, by phone or by e-mail. This is the equivalent of a carpenter having a saw and wood. Without the basic materials nothing will happen.

The **Fine Tools** are like the carpenter's blueprint, along with the fine shaping and design tools. These allow you to determine your goal, organize, plan, and follow up with your contacts. They are the relationship building tools that increase the power of your connections.

Collateral is your marketing materials. These are your "calling cards" that summarize the services you can provide to your potential client — the person who will eventually hire you.

The **Studio Extras** provide ambience, encouragement and the right environment to get the work done. A great woodworker works in a studio that inspires creativity — the same applies to you. Surround yourself with as many helpful extras that make this task as playful as possible, and help keep your eye on the ball.

The next activity — *Tool Kit Assembly* — will provide you with a simple process for assembling your tool kit. Once again, this may sound overly obvious, but it is an important concrete action that you need to take. When a carpenter gets prepared for a job, I assure you that the effective ones check before they go to make sure the hammers, nails, staple guns, and glue are in good supply and properly placed in the tool belt. It's a matter of efficiency, safety and responsiveness. I want you to be able to respond quickly to anything that comes your way, so go assemble that tool kit.

Activity 4

Tool Kit Assembly

GO

The tool kit on page 24 provides a checklist for organizing yourself. Below are some questions to help you identify your needs from the tool kit, including workspace, and the priorities you need to pay attention to.

STEPS

1. **Decide** if you are more scattered / spontaneous or organized / methodical.

   a. If organized, review the checklist, make sure you have the basics covered, and move on.

   b. If scattered, copy the checklist and put it in the 3-ring notebook you will purchase or find in your closet.

2. **Determine if you will work in the same place** all the time.

   a. If yes, set up your work station with everything you need.

   b. If no, pack a travel bag.

3. **Write down the attributes** of a good working environment for you and use this as your guide.

4. **As you know you,** is there anything special you need in your tool kit that will help you concentrate and stay up for this? (iPod? Favorite book? Inspirational quotes? etc.) Add to the list.

5. **Check off** each key item as you assemble it into your kit.

6. Keep **one** notebook or folder to organize yourself.

Start-up Essentials

There is one piece of your tool kit that you will need to develop now, if you don't have it already — your resume and a model for your cover letter. Of the two, the resume is by far the most important. But experience has taught me that opportunities pop up at the most surprising moments, and having the outline of a good cover letter ready to be tailored to a specific opportunity will save you time and spare you some stress.

You will find all the how-tos for resumes and cover letters in the *Resource Center* under *Job Search Stuff*. But just in case you already have both of these, please read the critical guidelines below, and if your resume isn't up to it, skip over to the *Resource Center* and spruce it up.

Like a fashion guru, I want to steer you in the direction of the absolute must haves in the resume world. They are:

Essential Resume Tips

1. It's short (one page for less than seven years experience).

2. It's simple, with lots of white space.

3. It includes a short summary of skills at the top.

There are two things to remember about resumes in the twenty-first century: 1) people don't read; and 2) computers scan for key words. Don't ever forget that this is marketing material — it's designed to put you in the best light possible, and to get people's attention quickly (and that doesn't mean neon or scented paper). We live in the age of fifteen-second commercials, and you want your fifteen seconds to count.

When it comes to cover letters, pretty much the same rules apply. This is your chance, though, to spice up the message with storytelling and some of your passion. Don't blow it by repeating your resume.

Another collateral tool is the cover e-mail. There is a fine art to well-crafted e-mails that people will actually read—accurately! This is the den of supreme skimming—so every word counts. At issue here is whether to make the e-mail your cover letter, or simply introduce the cover letter and resume as attachments. There are several "it depends" on this. You'll find those in the *Job Search Stuff* section of the *Resource Center*, along with some tips on crafting these e-mails. Bottom line: keep it "sweet and simple."

So as long as you have your tool kit set up, including your basic collateral, let's get back to the topic of connecting to people. Not too long ago, you made your *Coffee House Blueprint* with your initial ideas of what you might be interested in. Let's go back to that and get some action with it by starting the connecting process.

Networking 101

If you are great at making connections with people, then you may move through the next step quickly, or even move right past it. But before you make that decision, let's talk about what it means to make a connection. Even if you are comfortable interviewing people, I suggest you start here anyway. This is a new angle for you, as you prepare to choose your next opportunity on purpose.

Most of the time when people start reshaping their lives and looking for a job, they will tell you how important it is to *network*. They are absolutely right. And there's a *but*. If it's not authentic, don't bother. Authentic, to me, means working with and through other people, not using them as a stepping-stone for what you want. The connections you make today will somehow show up again in ten, twenty, forty years. Make 'em good, and make 'em mean something.

A contact in your network is someone who has useful information about the life and career you are pursuing. This isn't always, or even often, the name of a potential future boss. Only a handful of your conversations will get you to an interview. This is a step-by-step process of connecting into a web and building it. This "webbing" process will eventually connect you to the work of your dreams, if you let it. Pushing doesn't build friendly or helpful networks or webs. Drawing out does. Think of the very spider we identify with a web. They plant their starting spot and draw out from that spot, attaching to the next target. There's no pushing or forcing. It's organic.

This doesn't mean that every contact must become a long lost friend. It does mean, however, that every contact deserves your respect, your attention, and appropriate follow-through. This is another one of those things that sounds simple, but isn't always easy. When you have so much going on, especially when stressed to get a job, the little things (like a follow-up phone call) can sometimes fall off the list. This is where discipline counts.

Anyone you ask for help should be someone *you* would be willing to help too. You know the old saying, "What goes around, comes around." A contact can be anyone from a family member to your friend's boyfriend's boss — one of those six degrees of separation you don't know yet.

Note, though, that the farther away a contact is from knowing you, the weaker that connection is. This doesn't mean the friend's boyfriend won't mention your name to his boss — but it will be a very different conversation than if a close personal friend were vouching for you. On the other hand, if you're willing to pay some attention to the contacts you make and invest in the relationship building — then you can get a lot of mileage out of your contacts, even when they're five or six degrees away.

If you're comfortable talking to people, especially strangers, about what's really important to you, what you're good at, and what you love to do, then with this basic information in hand about networking, you're ready to go. If, on the other hand, you are shy, somewhat introverted, or slow to talk to new people, then you need to start the networking process in a much more comfortable arena. This next activity is aimed at you. But even if you are more outgoing you may want to try this. Remember, each climb is different, so starting at home is great for you too.

Start-at-home Networking. This idea of beginning networking at home came from an early interview I had with Sara. She was a college roommate of my daughter's and during a group discussion with about six graduating seniors, we started talking about the highs and lows of networking. Sara volunteered that she was quite shy, and had a lot of fears about talking to people about her career interests. She decided to practice on her aunt. At that point, Sara was not yet clear on her career interests, but she knew her aunt worked in marketing — an area that was close to her interests.

Sara got the whole discussion group turned on to her idea. Everyone in the group was impressed by what she did — a creative solution to a common dilemma. And everyone also felt like, "Duh, why didn't I think of that?!" Just reach out to someone you're comfortable talking with.

Sara did interview her aunt, and she was stunned to find out things she never knew about her aunt or the immensely fun work she was engaged in. She learned a lot on two fronts from the interview. First, she started learning how to interview someone, informally. She discovered that just talking about career aspirations helped get the momentum started.

Informal is the key — because that way she was natural, herself — no pretenses. Second, her aunt, someone who had just been there all her life, turned out to have experience she never would have imagined. She had made the assumption that no one in her family could possibly be useful to her. And not surprisingly, as assumptions often do, they proved her wrong.

Sara went on to discover her purpose. But it took her a couple of tries to get on the right path. She spent six months in her first job in medical public relations — which wasn't the best fit. She was in the right neighborhood — customer relations, but she needed more variety and more challenge. What it did do, though, was teach her to focus on what she really wanted. Her persistence paid off. Sara ended up working for a financial investment firm in New York City, where she now talks to new people every day.

The same steps are possible for you. Activity 5, shows you how to set up an information interview with someone either in your family or close to you. An information interview is exactly what it says — you interview someone for information about the career they are in. You pick someone who is working in an area close to your interests.

When you are networking, think *conversation*. It's an exchange of ideas that both helps you understand the career area, and helps the person you interview, a seasoned performer, validate his or her work, demonstrate pride, and serve as your supporter. Such exchanges are invaluable, and will lead you to the next best opportunity.

Activity 5, helps you set up, then gives you a very sturdy set of questions that are sure to get your information interview buzzing. You will draw on this process many times, so relax, learn and enjoy.

 Activity 5

First Contact: Interviewing an Experienced Friend

 GO

Interview someone you are very comfortable with, who has many years in her career, and therefore qualifies as a practiced, world-wise person. Even if the person you interview isn't in a job exactly like what you think you want, do it for the experience. An Information Interview Notes worksheet follows the steps below to help you stay organized (page 34).

I'm offering a sample script below as a conversation starter, but please make it your own, use what works for you, leave the rest behind. **Do,** however, use the interview questions. They are proven and powerful.

STEPS

1. Find the right contact

- Talk to your closest friends and family about the list you made on the *Coffee House Blueprint*.

- Ask them to help you identify a friend, family member, or work colleague that you already know, would feel comfortable talking to, and has some background or enthusiasm about your areas of interest.

- Ask your friend or family to talk to this person and let them know you will be calling. Make sure the person knows you want to talk about her career and your career interests.

2. Make the connection

- Make the phone call and ask for a half hour to talk about your interests. Here's a sample of the conversation:

  "Hi Aunt Jane, it's Roger. I'm doing some career research, and I would love to talk to you about what you do and your career. I think you could help me think through some of my options. I'd like to do it in person, so when would you be available, and where would it be easiest for us to get together?" (If this person is across the country, resist the urge to have the conversation right then and there. Schedule it, at least for the following day. It's always good to give people a chance to think a little in advance of the conversation.)

- Send a reminder e-mail or give a call the day before the interview.

3. Hold the conversation

- Once you are ready to get started, if you know the person well, spend a few minutes catching up. Don't let your time slip away, though, and after five or so minutes explain what you want to talk about. Here's how it could go:

"Aunt Jane, as you know, I'm starting a career search. I'm figuring out what I want to focus on. I'm here today to hear your story about your career so I can get some ideas on how to approach my search. I just have a few questions, so let me go over them with you and then we'll start with the first one. Here are the basic things I'd like to know about:

    1) What brought you to this career?
    2) What is it like on a day-to-day basis?
    3) What keeps you doing this?
    4) If you could do something else for a living, what would it be?

Now — let's start with the first question:

    1) *What brought you to this career?* (Coax her to include her background, work history, skills and talents, and interests.)

    2) *What is it like on a day-to-day basis?* (Tell me about the highlights and the challenges, the exciting parts, the annoying parts and the boring parts, and what you spend most of your time doing.)

    3) *What keeps you doing this?* (You can talk about things like your passions and interests, your needs, how you contribute, the people and environment you work in.)

    4) *If you could do something else for a living, what would it be?*

- Just listen — no note taking. This is a pure conversation. You'll write notes after Aunt Jane, your "first contact" interview, leaves, with one exception — the next bullet.

- Ask: Any ideas of who else I could talk to? Would you refer me? Take notes here!

Information Interview Notes

Referrals
Name, Phone, email

Name of Interviewee: Date

1) What brought you to this career?
   (interests, needs, skills, background)

2) What is it like on a day-to-day basis?
   (tasks, positive and negative, variety)

3) What keeps you doing this? (passion,
   need, skill, investment)

4) If you could do something else for a
   living, what would it be? (similar? Different?)

Date thank you sent: _____

4. Follow-up

- As soon as you've left, pull over somewhere, then pull out your notebook and write your notes now — impressions, ideas for searching, what surprised you, what validated your interests.

- Hand write a thank you note and send it within twenty-four hours. (I'll talk more about this shortly.)

Celebrate! A simple step like this will start opening doors. If you grab a latte, I'll be there in spirit, "clinking" my paper cup to yours.

Finding a Mentor

In short order you have made significant progress! You have made a first pass at defining your areas of interest, you've gotten organized, and have already begun the discussion and interviewing process. A little structure can take you a long way. So let's keep moving. There are two more parts to the beginning — *Finding a Mentor* and *Building a Plan*. The plan comes last because you will have much of the thinking done to start it — budding career ideas, your hopes and your roadblocks, and people lined up who can help you. So let's go find a mentor.

First, let me define what I mean by a mentor. A mentor is someone more experienced than you in life and the workplace, whom you trust and respect, and can speak with easily about what is important to you. I suggest you find at least one such person. I expect you will talk to friends and peers — and they will help you immensely through this process. But a more senior advisor, who can be more objective, will round out your support team.

No one does anything meaningful alone. I serve as your process guide. Besides me, though, you need people who can engage with you in dialogue and give you immediate feedback. These mentors will listen to you, make you feel good about yourself, but also challenge you, and hold the mirror up to you. They will say, "Look at what you've got going; look at what's missing; what do you want to do about it?"

Usually I advise people to find a mentor (or two) who can play two roles: the supportive role, and the challenger role. The big question is: do I know someone who can fill this role well? And what, exactly, does that look, sound and feel like?

As you identify your mentor, you will have to use both your head and your heart. Use your head to find someone who is objective and insightful and your heart to see who you can trust. Below are some tips on what to look for. Then, in the activity that follows you will make a list of five to seven possible people who could be your mentor. Once you boil that list down to one or two, you're going to pick up the phone and invite him to mentor you.

Tips for Finding Mentors

1. Does this person know me well enough to give objective, honest feedback?

2. Do I respect this person's values and way of living? (Work / life balance, honesty, caring, respect, responsibility.)

3. Does this person have extensive life and workplace experience? (Has he handled excitement and disappointment, promotion and rejection, balancing family, work and hobbies?)

4. Will he support me in the highs and the lows?

5. Will he be available for phone calls, e-mails and occasional hour-long conversations?

Activity *6*

Possible Mentors

Identify possible mentors.

1. **Review the tips** list above.

2. **Consult** with parents, family or friends to get input on your choices. Your mentor can be a family member, even parents, *if* they can be objective enough (big if).

3. **Brain dump** here all the possible names. (Could the person you did the First Contact conversation with be that person? Keep this as simple as you can.)

      1.

      2.

      3.

      4.

      5.

      6.

      7.

4. **Prioritize the list**—just in case you need to go beyond the top two choices to find a mentor who is available for you now.

5. **Make your selection.** When selecting, don't forget you want to be challenged!

Now that you've made the selection, the next activity provides you a sample script of what to say when you invite this person. Take a walk now or go do a favorite exercise. While you're doing this, think about why you picked this person, so you can be ready to explain that if you're asked. You may want to review the tips, and during your walk or workout think about how your mentors meet those criteria.

NOTE: Resist the urge to skip these movement breaks. They really do matter in making this process work. Neuroscience has repeatedly shown that the best way to activate the brain is not Sudoku or electronic brain games, but physical activity. Nike is truly on to something with their "Just Do It!" tagline.

Once back from getting some physical activity, use the script below to help you get started.

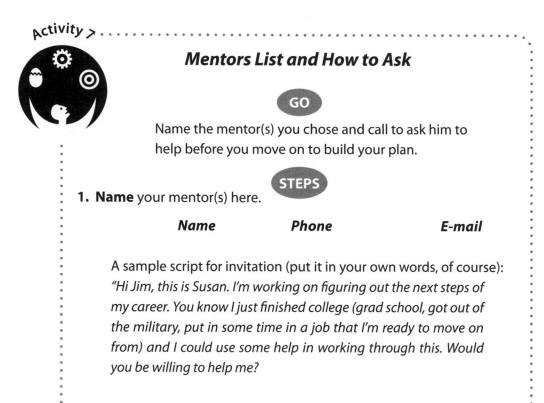

Activity >

Mentors List and How to Ask

GO

Name the mentor(s) you chose and call to ask him to help before you move on to build your plan.

STEPS

1. **Name** your mentor(s) here.

Name	Phone	E-mail

A sample script for invitation (put it in your own words, of course): *"Hi Jim, this is Susan. I'm working on figuring out the next steps of my career. You know I just finished college (grad school, got out of the military, put in some time in a job that I'm ready to move on from) and I could use some help in working through this. Would you be willing to help me?*

I'm asking for your time, your ear, and your feedback. Specifically, there may be some short e-mails or phone calls, and some longer visits of about an hour, face to face if we can, to hash through some bigger questions and get your honest feedback.

Most of all, I need you to be honest with me, tell me what you see and offer input and advice. What do you think? THANKS!"

2. **Make the calls now.** Get your mentor in place before you move ahead. Getting him involved early helps him feel like a part of creating success with you.

3. **What if he says no?** First of all, consider it a gift — this was not the right person for this time. You have two options. If you picked two, you can proceed with the second mentor. If both said no, then move down your list to the next person. Try hard to get at least one person. While I can offer you a lot, it's helpful to have someone closer to you who can work with your immediate needs.

Building a Plan

Now you are almost at the end of the beginning. This is where you will get familiar with all the elements of making a plan to change your life. You won't have everything in play yet, but let's move anyway. It will help you know all the items you need for this climb — from nourishment to tools, and from necessities to niceties.

Let's lay out the plan. For goodness sake don't over-think this. You may be a spreadsheet person or a sticky note person — both work. Don't worry how your neighbor does it — this is YOUR plan. I'll give you some very specific guidelines to make it work.

Activity 8A

A Plan with Kick

Part A — Project Plan

GO

Organize yourself with an overall Project Plan, and a Contact List. Part A guides you in using the Project Plan, and Part B guides you in constructing your Contact List.

STEPS

1. OVERVIEW

- Put your name and today's date at the top (the plan is on page 44). Describe what this project is about, as much as you know right now. You will be refining this, but give it a placeholder for now. Mine was "Get Susan a published book and great Web site on helping people choose and get the life they deserve." Rudimentary, but it worked for me.

- Identify the goals you have so far. They may be broad now — like move to X city, or get a job in X field. More on this later.

2. TIMELINE

- **Desired start date for new job/move/opportunity:** Be realistic on time frames — launching a career, even a first job, can take a while — depending on how clear you are on what you want, and how flexible you are. Up to three months is not unusual (from the date you do something like this, which shows you're committed), although you never know!

- **Backup plan:** It's always good to have a fallback plan. What if you don't find a job that matches you by your desired start date? Can you work part-time for a while, as a barista, a night stocker at a store, wait tables? What about a temp job? Temping is a great way to get exposed to different work environments, and you're learning about what you want (and don't want) while you're earning some money.

3. RESOURCES

- **Support Team**: Write down the names of your mentors, friends, colleagues, family who can help you.

- **Collateral**: Keep track of the document names (resume, cover letter, etc.) and where you are keeping them (laptop, flash drive, hard copy in folder, etc.)

- **Financial**: Anything else that will help support you during the search time? A place to stay (especially important if you move to a new city), extra money. Any other Plan B kinds of things you need to consider? Insurance? Rainy day money?

4. ENERGY

- **Motivation:** Some background: Your spirit and energy level are key to success. I am a pianist, and I'm always interested in how musicians become accomplished in their fields. I recently read that it's 10,000 hours of practice that make a virtuoso — not just special talent! In other words — if you want it badly enough, you'll do what it takes. At the heart of this must be what motivates *you*.

- **Physical:** Movement is a requirement of any great achievement. This is more than nice to have, it's a necessity. For your body to serve you well, it needs to be active. Create a workout schedule, join a team, or plan for a walk every day. I will continue to pinpoint moments during our work together when you need to get up and move, in order to process what you are working on.

- **Motivation Task 1:** Find a Pet Project.
  - Pet Project: Side by side with your life and work goal, this project will be something concrete that will allow you to see progress.

It can range from learning to cook, to running a marathon, to building a cabinet. There is nothing like seeing the progress of building something to boost this enterprise of *Choosing on Purpose!* And the added bonus is it gives you a great reason to invest your time and energy in recreation — the activities that quite literally re-create you!

- **Motivation Task 2:** Find a theme song and a mascot.
  - Song: Please don't tell me that you've never cranked up the sound on the car radio and belted one out. This is all about that. Use your theme song any way it suits you. Some people start the day with it, others use it to get them motivated when they are dragging.
  - Mascot: Find an item that describes you and/or your situation well right now. I am especially fond of toys for this — they make great metaphors and remind you to have fun and stay light on your feet. Identify attributes you share with your toy or object.
  - Write how the mascot describes you well:
  - Place it on your desk: Place it where you'll see it every day as you work. It will remind you of what you have to offer — including a sense of humor!

- **On the form, write what you will commit to and tell your friends.**

A Note on Pet Projects

I have found over the years that having a side project that requires you to exert some discipline, and often some physical effort, is good for the soul, the brain and one's ego. I learned this from my husband. When he was laid off in the early '90s, he started a deck-building project. At the time, I thought he was nuts. We had two young kids, and not a lot of extra cash floating around.

As it turns out, he was a very wise man indeed. The physical labor helped him work off the anger from the layoff and the stress of the job hunt. And the steady sense of accomplishment, as he saw concrete progress on the deck, bolstered his confidence in the job search process. Wouldn't you know that the deck was just about finished when he was offered the job he ended up accepting. Even better, his patience and ability to put his whole self in the process — body, mind and spirit, turned up the work that so matched his purpose, he has been doing it ever since.

As a result, I have been recommending that people take on a Pet Project during this major change time. It works miracles! While something physical like building, training for a competition or finally cleaning the basement helps with the physical release, knitting a scarf or building a train set will do the trick too.

A little discipline goes a long way. I've kept a sign on my desk for years that says *Discipline is the price you pay for freedom*. I can't tell you how often I've needed that reminder. Whether it's a checklist or follow-up reminders — this is what makes your world sane and decent at a time like this — doing what you say you're going to do, and being responsible (think *response-able*).

My Project Plan

(Customize Each Line)

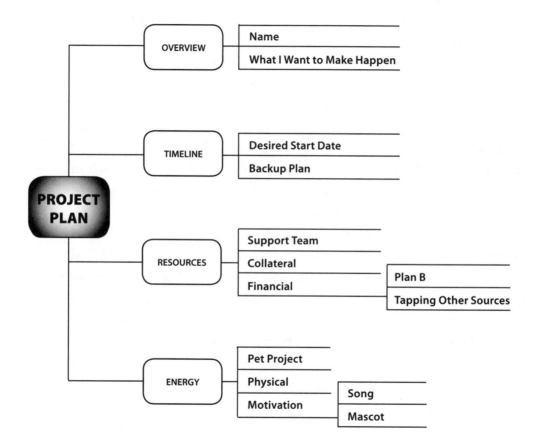

Moving on to Part B
Contact List for Choosing on Purpose

Now let's turn to the second form (page 47), which is simply an expanded TO DO list. It focuses on two things that you will be scheduling and working on during the *Discovery* process — contacts, and your research. You're about to enter a cycle of think a little, do a little — over and over. The thinking part comes in your reflection on interests, purpose, and possibilities. The doing part comes in talking to people, many of them, until the right contact opens the right opportunity. Your TO DO list, therefore, will circle around the networking, connecting and follow-up process. This, in turn, will create further requirements for research and reflection. The tracking worksheet (your TO DO list) has these elements:

CONTACT LIST

Contact Name	Phone	E-mail / Snail Mail	Focus	Addl. Research	Date	Follow-up

This is one form you really *need*. Organize it any way you like. Either keep track of it by hand in your notebook, or set it up as a spreadsheet. Just use it. You will be amazed at how many details there are to track. You already have an entry — your First Contact interview — and you can add your mentor.

Activity 8B

Part B — Contact List

GO

This form (page 47) is mostly self-explanatory. The big issue here is being diligent in keeping it up.

STEPS

Some hints on use:

- **Contact Name**: Make sure you ask for proper spelling of the name. Also identify who referred you, and the kind of contact this is (personal, information interview, job interview).

- **Phone**: Get office, cell, and home if appropriate.

- **E-mail/Snail Mail**: Again spelling, and full snail mail address.

- **Focus**: Identify what you are discussing with this person, such as what company, industry, and career path. You may be looking at several different career paths, and it's easy to lose track of who you talked to about what.

- **Additional Research**: Identify what else you need to find out about, like online research about a company, research into a job area you are not familiar with (more on this later — also in the *Picture Work You Love* section of the *Resource Center*), industries in certain parts of the country, etc.

- **Date**: The date of the contact — whether meeting or phone call, or important e-mail.

- **Follow-up**: Keep track of when you need to re-contact this person, what you promised to do, when you sent a thank you note, or even if this contact is closed for you.

Contact Name	Phone	E-mail / Snail Mail	Focus	Additional Research	Date	Follow-up

CONTACT LIST

Stay with the Program. As tempting as it may be to skip over some of the activities above, stick with the program. These steps have traveled across many projects and helped people not only focus on key success elements, but kept their moods up during lulls and setbacks.

Signs That You Are Implementing Your Plan

There are a handful of things that create the evidence that you're serious and excited about committing to this search. Here are some of those signs:

1. Clear Expectations. You can identify without hesitation the expectations you have for your search and exploration process. In the beginning they may be mostly about doing your research, meeting with people, and focusing on your goal to find the work you love. As you progress, though, you will get clearer on the kind of work you want, the kinds of relationships you want, and where you can make that all happen.

2. Commitment: You Spend the Time. A full-time job search equals about five hours a day, five days a week. You may think that you need to be on this 24/7, but the reality is you want to pace yourself. First, you will spend time waiting for people to respond to you. Second, you want to have enough work ideas and people to connect with to keep you always having another bit of research or follow-up to do, as well as space in your schedule to meet with people.

You also need time to think broadly about your purpose and the people in your life. And you need to exercise, and to work on your Pet Project. This re-creation time is part of the plan. Your brain is doing a lot of reorganizing as you determine what is important to you, and the kinds of opportunities that fit you.

You can, of course, spend more time — but still, pace yourself. You're learning about all the things that will contribute to a full life. A lot is changing right now. This is like writing a book. Sometimes you'll get a block, and you need other activities to help you get unblocked — like your Pet Project, or exercise. This is an ebb and flow kind of endeavor.

A part-time job search (when you're working full-time or close to it) requires at least half as much time as a full-time search, when you're not working another job. This means you'll be putting ten to fifteen hours per week into it. You're looking at a couple of hours a night, two or three nights a week, and about eight hours across the weekend.

It will probably take a little longer to find a job, simply because you don't have as much time to schedule as many information interviews as someone looking full-time. But as long as you're able to make a living, it's worth working at it a little more slowly to get the next opportunity that fits you well and feels purposeful.

3. Using Your Mentors. When you ask for help, you know you're serious. It also shows an earnest desire to learn and grow. Other people love being around someone who is growing — it's exciting.

4. Being Adventurous. It takes courage to pursue a future that matches who you are, your skills and your passions. There are many pressures to conform. Your plan succeeds to the extent you are willing to go outside your comfort zone and stretch yourself — be it emotionally, physically, intellectually, or socially. For some, it may be picking up the phone and talking to a stranger. For others, it may be the willingness to learn a skill you believed was truly outside your scope. And the adventure keeps you riveted to pursuing the process.

A Word on Etiquette

I know it sounds old-fashioned, but it's important to consider how to be thoughtful of others as you contact, connect, and follow up. It all boils down to doing what you say you will do. When people help you, they want to know how the story ends. Don't forget to tell people what you did! As simple as this sounds, it makes a big impact on people and their future willingness to help you or others.

What I mean is, if you get some coaching from a mentor, and follow up on that tip — write her and let her know you got something done. It shows progress, honors the help you are getting, and lets that person know how committed you are. This is that old *Discipline is the price you pay. . .* thing. It really works! All that is required of you is a two-line e-mail, or a thirty-second phone call. And the mentor's or contact's words of encouragement will help keep your mood up and confidence strong.

The other big issue is saying thank you. Every information interview, every job interview merits a thank you. And that especially includes showing gratitude and appreciation through such "old-fashioned" notions as hand-written thank you notes. You will be amazed at how impressed people are in this day of electronic correspondence to get a hand-written note. It shows respect, attention to detail, and the gift of your time and reflection.

Etiquette, in the form of follow-through and expressed gratitude, makes you stand out. And this is the time to stand out! The *Resource Center* on *Job Search Stuff* can help you with suggestions on writing thoughtful thank yous. But never forget to put yourself into these notes. It's not about polish — it's about authenticity.

Bring It In. Now you have a plan. This is the bedrock of your search. You have identified a mentor and begun your outreach program. Use these tools like a carpenter uses a blueprint — checking them often to ensure the excellence of your outcome.

Heads Up. The next step is to get you grounded in the WHAT–WHERE–WHO questions of life. So let's turn to these three ways to know what you want, so you can start doing it.

3

Asking Key Questions

You are definitely in *Launch* mode now! You've put a stake in the ground, so let's look at what brought you to this book at this point in your life. Before you write an answer to that, take the question with you through five minutes of movement. Take a short walk, or turn on the radio and boogie a little, shoot some hoops, or check the *Resource Center* on *Movement* for other suggestions.

Go. Move. Now. Think: what brought you here now? You may be wondering, why even ask this now, when I am already into it. It's like taking a deep breath to clear your head. Step away, get some perspective — feel confident, purposeful about your next steps.

Activity 9

Why This, Why Now?

GO

Name your thoughts and feelings as you finish the
Launch process and begin the *Discovery* phase.

STEPS

1. **Briefly describe** what brought you to this book at this time in
   your life.

2. **How are you feeling about these needs and wishes right now?**
   Choose one word or write in your word.

   Hopeful   Determined   Worried   Excited   Undaunted

   Anxious   Other _____

3. **Thoughts?**

You are poised for action. You've acknowledged your distractions, become
familiar with my coaching method, and put your first thoughts down about
why this, why now. Reread your letter from Activity 1, *Moving Towards What
You Want* (page 15), and if it makes sense (and it's not to a boss), send it.
Keep that fresh in your mind as we explore the three questions of life and
the choice-making process.

Checking in with Yourself

Your situation today results from stacks and stacks of little decisions you have made over your lifetime. Unfortunately, we usually don't recognize the impact of these decisions, and wake up one morning sad or surprised at where we are. The fact is, you are where you are because of choices you have made in your life. You can point and blame all you want, but your life today results from your choices yesterday.

So from here on, sit up and start checking in and paying attention to the choices you make. For example, if you've ever complained about a poor test grade, have you ever really looked at the choices that led up to it? Did you go to class? Did you do your homework and reading? Did you ask enough questions? Did you party the night before? Did you cram? Each choice influenced the outcome.

You can change your choice-making process today. In fact, if you are this far, you already have. Small choice by small choice, you weave a web. You've paid attention to your distractions and noted what brought you here. So you've set in motion the process of paying attention.

Let me introduce you to how we will be doing the *Discovery* process. First, I want to acquaint you with a reminder that will pop up from time to time throughout the rest of the book. Look at the image on the right. It is your prompt to observe, to shine a light on, and to ask yourself — Where am I? What's the situation and how am I feeling about it? — and What now? What's my next move and how do I want to handle myself?

PAY ATTENTION
Gut instinct

What's your next move?

The more observant you become of your own thoughts, feelings, and actions, the better you will be able to make clear choices, unencumbered by the weight of the melodrama or anxiety of the moment. So I encourage you to actually stop when you see this circle, take a brief time-out, and examine the issue at hand.

Your New Choices in Today's World

Let's prepare for the *Discovery* process by taking stock. Look back for a moment and position yourself. You're preparing to make choices about your life. At the opening of the twentieth century, however, most people in the world did not believe they had the opportunity to even ask questions about their future. They followed in the footsteps of their forefathers and mothers, working the same livelihoods, marrying the people they were matched to, and living in the region where they were born. Few dreamed of choosing something different, usually because crossing geographical and social barriers was too demanding, and just not even imagined, much less attempted.

Much has changed in the last 100 years. Cars and trains and planes have opened new vistas. Public education has widened imaginations, and the relaxing of social constraints has connected people across cultural, ethnic and geographic boundaries. On top of that, along came technology to diminish distance and expand information through the instant Internet.

In *The World is Flat*, Tom Friedman talked about how open our world is today, how anyone can work anywhere in the world, and how work is 24/7, crossing international boundaries. Today people compete for jobs not just in their hometown, but all across the globe, as formerly third world people become more educated and available to contribute in the global marketplace. In particular, Friedman highlighted how many more choices we have as a result. Today, there are fewer barriers than ever. Technology brings the world to our doorstep, and opportunity lies everywhere. What is a chooser to do?

Three "W" Questions

The first thing a chooser does is narrow the scope of options without closing the pathways to opportunities. It's a both/and approach to life, rather than either/or. It's best summed up by a concept coined by Fred Rogers, the famous public television producer of children's programs.

Fred, better known as "Mr. Rogers" (yes, I know this takes you back to first grade, but stay with me), was a pioneer in the new technology of television in the 1950s. As a young man attending college in the 1940s, how could he possibly imagine a lifelong career in television—an emerging technology? Nevertheless, the technology found him, as new programs were seeking people skilled in production. With a degree in music and experience producing musical performances, Rogers was primed for the new media. And because he had confidence in his intuition—the knowledge of his heart—and his skills, he was able to respond to opportunity when it knocked.

He believed the best way to manage transitions was through something he called *Guided Drift*. This guidance, as he saw it, comes from your choices; the drift arises from an openness to really *NOTICE* what appears on your path, because anything is possible. His experience of drifting into that new medium of the twentieth century is so like yours—coming of age in a world full of fast-changing technology. Your dreams, like his, will be shaped by the environment of your time. So I adopt *Guided Drift*—a both/and approach to shaping your life.

Guided Drift

The notion of drift implies an anchor point—your values, hopes and dreams. If you think *Guided Drift* is a romantic notion of a past generation, read what Steve Jobs, the founder of Apple, has to say about his own career (from a commencement speech at Stanford in 2005):

> "You can't connect the dots looking forward; you can only connect them looking backwards. So you have to trust that the dots will somehow connect in your future. You have to trust in something—your gut, destiny, life, karma, whatever. This approach has never let me down, and it has made all the difference in my life . . .
>
> "Your time is limited, so don't waste it living someone else's life. Don't be trapped by dogma—which is living with the results of

PAY ATTENTION
Intuition Rules

What's your next move?

other people's thinking. Don't let the noise of others' opinions drown out your own inner voice. And most important, have the courage to follow your heart and intuition. They somehow already know what you truly want to become. Everything else is secondary."

Paying attention to *Guided Drift* led Fred Rogers from an early career goal of flying airplanes to the destiny of influencing the values of a generation of American children. It led Steve Jobs from being fired from the company he created to getting re-employed several years later and changing the way people connect and create through computers and devices like the iPod. *Guided Drift* is alive and well.

The *Guided Drift* approach helps you navigate your life by asking three questions you will answer again and again over your lifetime:

- What do I want to be?
- Where do I want to be?
- Who do I want to be with?

There is, of course, a parcel of universal questions about human existence (like Why are we here? Where did we come from?), but those are philosophical and spiritual ponderings for another time. Important though they are, we are here to focus on you and what you want to make happen today. So let's look at what comprises each of these questions.

What do I want to be?

What am I good at? What do I love to do? What kind of career do I want? What values do I live by? What hobbies and interests will occupy my time? How do I want to balance leisure time, work time and family time? What is my passion? What skills do I bring to the table? What can I contribute to the world? What is my calling?

Where do I want to be?

What kind of activity do I want surrounding me? The pulse of the city? The calm of the small town? Do my interests draw me to a particular geography? Climate? Political environment? Emotional environment? Do I want to live near family and friends? Is there a particular environment or headspace calling me?

Who do I want to be with?

Who brings out the best in me? What kind of friends and family do I want around me? Who do I turn to for support, guidance and feedback? What kind of people do I want to work with? Who makes me a better person? Who do I want actively in my life?

One Question at a Time. These three simple questions form the core of how we lead our lives with intention. There is no doubt they are inter-related, that each one affects the other. Yet, trying to force an answer to all of them at once is not effective either. I want to uncomplicate the searching process for you, and the best way to do that is to take one step at a time. My goal is to give you enough guidance so that when you drift into a great opportunity, you'll recognize it and take off.

It helps, of course, to know what is important to you, what you value. Think about what you value and what you spend your time on. Do you see yourself as a humanitarian? As an influencer and controller? As an analytical person? As someone who values organization? As someone artistic, with good taste? Or are you very practical? Free-thinking and independent? Deeply spiritual?

If you can identify two drivers from this list that describe you better than the rest, then you have a pretty good grasp of your values. The ability to see what values, passions, abilities and needs drive you, helps you dive into the questions. If you're struggling, go to the *Resource Center* in Section 5, *WHAT – WHERE – WHO Now?* There you will find some help on exploring your values more deeply.

Good Questions Lead to Good Choices. It sounds too simple, doesn't it? I'm advising you to sit down and just ask yourself what you want to do. It's true, however, that in order to choose well, you have to pose the questions well. You will need some preparation for that. I prepare all my clients for coaching by reminding them about spring training.

We get so wrapped up in living that we forget to stop and go back to basics. In spring training, the best baseball players in the world spend weeks hitting, throwing and catching — back to the basics. Finding success and happiness asks you to do the same. You stay good at your game by mastering the basic moves of asking good questions, making good choices, and taking action.

What to Do with the 3Ws

You can put the 3Ws to work in three key ways. Three is a great number. With three legs you can balance a stool, with three balance points you can execute a headstand, and with three strands you can braid a strong rope (not to mention the spiritual implications of three). Let's examine three moves, Ask — Choose — Act, that drive your discovery of the 3Ws.

Move 1: ASK. Get curious. Snoop around in your own business, finding out what suits you, what drives you, what pleases you. And keep asking as life moves you forward. Things change, and the answers evolve over time. As you keep asking questions, you get good at asking the right questions about what you want and where you stand. You can only get the right answer if you ask the right question. Never stop asking.

The root of life questioning starts with "What else is possible?" Just saying the possible out loud starts to get you out of your rut. Feel good about the possibility questions you have already answered. Shortly, we will put you into more training on that. But first, let's look at Move 2: Choose — the key to shaping a life of purpose.

Move 2: CHOOSE. Learn to lose your fear of making choices. Much of our overload today comes from the notion that it is a great thing to "keep our options open." Not true. While there is a time for this, mostly we need to get better at cutting out options. It's that notion of *Guided Drift* again. All options open is sheer floating, but posing a question and choosing a response — that's guided action. Drift indicates an anchor point. Choosing always comes from the anchor of your values. That's why we talk about drifting and not floating — there is a home base we are tied to, which we also refer to as your gut feeling, your intuition, indeed, your purpose.

Choosing eliminates noise, places us on a path, and starts moving us towards results. Above all, once we make a choice, we can <u>do</u> something about it. Not making a decision is risky business. It gives us time to let our distractions become our focal point, and can stick us in continuous loops or keep us in hibernation. At times, this behavior pushes others to choose for us, and then we become victims of indecision.

You identified some critical loops and distractions already. The choice you made to pick up this book has reaped benefits. You are thinking now about where you are, how you ask questions (if at all) and whether they lead you to making active and appropriate choices. So now that you have chosen this coaching process, you are already experiencing Move 3 — you are engaged. But let's look at action a little more closely.

Move 3: ACT. Choosing means nothing if you don't act on it. Motion forward is required at this point. It's why I asked you to start the process, even without all your thinking completed. Movement starts momentum — and once you have it, it's easier to keep going. So all the tools and tips are meant to keep you acting.

Sean's story helps illuminate this whole 3W and Ask — Choose — Act thing. By way of introduction, Sean has spent his first few years after college searching for that match between talent and trade. With an American studies major from Dickinson College, and a career in both high school and college as a varsity athlete, he brought variety and breadth of experience to his search. With that, though, came little focus, except for his great passion for being part of a team, encouraging teammates, and thinking strategically about how to reach the goal.

For a while, Sean struggled solely with trying to figure out his WHAT. Through our conversations, and lots of purposeful reflecting, though, he realized that what he needed was to focus first on WHERE. He started his career working in an environment that didn't bring out the best in him. His first choice after college was to work in Washington, D.C. — a place that many peers on the East Coast saw as a great starter city for careers. Sean had done an internship in environmental policy there, and thought that sounded good.

But there are other sides of Sean that couldn't be well accommodated by working "inside the beltway" in D.C. His love of the outdoors, the environment — a hiker and skier — created a calling and a mindset that was far from D.C. WHERE was the next question he decided to answer. He ended up creating a true adventure for himself by moving to Denver after two years in D.C. — with no job, and just a bunk to sleep on at a friend's house. He embraced the adventure — especially finding the best 3W question for him as the starting point.

His adventure has been particularly poignant because he didn't give up on the discovery process. Instead, he paid even closer attention to what makes him tick, and had the guts to try out a new WHERE to help him grow. He's living proof that you can take a leap and let *Guided Drift* take over, because he definitely landed on his feet. We'll talk more about his landing later. But for now, notice that zeroing in on a good starting 3W question, and following through with it — in other words, making a decision — pays off.

Asking Good Questions in Life: What to Do. The fact is, everybody needs something to do in this world. With something to do, we feel plugged into the human network, and have a sense of what gets done because we're here. Without it, we're lost. It is the complement of *What to Be*.

Jon Kabat-Zinn, a pioneer in guiding people towards mindful endeavors and away from stress, speaks of it in a slightly different way. He asks us to ponder what is our Job on this planet, with a capital J? At the heart of the matter, what can you make happen that won't happen unless you take responsibility for it? This can range from the simple to the sublime, whether it's an elder in your family who takes pride in keeping the kitchen clean, as my ninetysomething mother does, or keeping patient data bases running for hospitals, as my husband does. Each is taking responsibility and making a difference.

That's why we spend a lot of energy on the questions what to be and what to do. As much as I would like to tell you that if you simply ask, "What do I want?" the answer will appear, for most of us a little searching is required.

I don't want you to overdo this searching, though. I was recently working on a farm (my family belongs to a farm co-op that requires service hours), and the farmer commented that every year, no matter where he plants the cucumbers or the potatoes, the potato beetles find the potatoes, and the cucumber beetles find the cucumbers. If beetles can find their target like magnets to the source, then surely each of us can find our purpose as well. The trick is getting out of our own way by asking questions and making choices.

Bring It In. We've talked about a lot of things, from *Guided Drift* to everybody needing "something to do." Most importantly, I introduced you to the 3Ws of life and how to discover the answers to the questions they pose. What you think may be your dream right now may reshape itself as you get better and better at answering questions with deliberate choices.

Heads Up. We're moving on to Phase II — *Discovery*. This is where we'll dig far enough into understanding your Job with a capital J to get you out talking to more people. It's a just-in-time approach that will get your information interviews and prospects flowing.

Phase II: DISCOVERY

Seeing Possibilities

Exploring

I f you're going to land the opportunity that fits you well for right now, it helps to know what you want. I'm talking about more than a job — I'm talking about building a repertoire of experience and skills that allows you to do what you love, so you can love what you do. Call it purpose, passion, destiny, or indeed, your calling — this is what allows you to lead a balanced, rich and rewarding life.

So, how do you make this happen if you're really not sure what that calling is? Simple. You assemble your gear and set out on an exploration trip. You determine how far and how long you want to go. I'm going to walk you through the basics of getting some initial answers on the WHAT – WHERE – WHO of your life. I'll also give you tips and tools to dig deeper in the *Resource Center* under *WHAT-WHERE-WHO Now?*

My goal is to get you enough to get going, without overwhelming you with too much soul searching. This is a fine balance of knowing enough, then trying something out. The best analogy I have is from a trip my family took to Mexico when my kids were little. A friend of ours took us on a hiking expedition in the foothills of the Sierra Madre Mountains. He told us there was a legend that bandits had hidden a treasure of Spanish gold in the area, and for years his family had been scouting the terrain, narrowing down the areas it could be hidden.

Like the bandit treasure hunt, you do enough work to get you closer for now, and continue to build your skills and your focus as you go along. What I loved about the treasure hunt in Mexico was how much our friends delighted in the search, without being obsessed by finding the treasure instantly. And it was fun! Like a scene out of a movie, we off-roaded in the desert, scrub brush, cactus and all, in a vintage World War II jeep, then jumped out and climbed with our backpacks and pickaxes. I want you to feel the same way.

Just as my friends had faith that their experience would lead them to the treasure eventually, so can you. And just like them, enjoy the discovery process! Every trip was one more piece of information, and one step closer to the gold (which I think was more about the experience than the coins).

WHERE and WHO:
Creating Culture and Environment

Before we start searching for the WHAT, though, we're going to focus on the WHERE-WHO. Often, we emphasize figuring out the WHAT, and forget to consider that the WHERE-WHO elements complete and balance our lives. An important part of creating possibilities is seeing who you're doing it with and where you're doing it. What's the fun of creating new possibilities without someone to share it with, in an environment that's inviting? The WHERE-WHO of your life makes the WHAT worth doing.

In fact, Richard Florida, in *Who's Your City,* contends that WHERE is the first, and most important question you can ask:

" . . . it's clear that many elements of a happy life — how much we make, how much we learn, how healthy we are, how stressful we feel, the job opportunities we have, and the people we meet — are in large part determined by where we live. Place plays a fundamental role in our endeavors to be happy. In many ways, it is the precursor to everything else."

> "Place plays a fundamental role in our endeavors to be happy."
> – Richard Florida

As you consider the WHERE-WHO, start thinking about the kinds of people and places that make you happy. We're really talking about the environment, the feel, the gut sensation of being able to relax and be challenged, as well as get crazy and just enjoy life. So environment and culture are central to figuring out how to be satisfied and happy with the WHAT of your life.

Over the years in my corporate consulting life I dealt a lot with corporate culture change. I learned that cultures don't change very rapidly or very often, unless you work deliberately and consistently at it. Look at simple, mechanical transactions, like using ATMs or downloading music. In both cases, it took a few years for people to adapt — and these were more convenient changes! On the more complex side, think about the changes a couple goes through when bringing home a new baby, or what parents and kids go through when departing for college or moving far away.

You're creating your life, your culture and your environment right now. In doing so, you're taking into consideration WHO is important to you and WHERE you want to be. So take an active hand in creating your culture and setting the environment and the tone of your life. Don't just accept whatever is out there. Pay attention. What might be hiding from you that is really going to get you excited?

PAY ATTENTION
What's in hiding?

What's your next move?

By the way, one of the great things I learned in corporate America is that the definition of culture is really simple. Culture is the way we do things around here. Think about when you were a kid. You'd visit the Jones house and everything would be neat as a pin, dinner always served at the same time, everything was clip-clip, tick-tock. Then you'd go into the Berg house, and well, everything was kind of free, dust bunnies on the floor, toys in the hall, and dinner came when it came. Maybe one house was quiet, the other rowdy. That's what we're talking about when we talk about culture.

What kind of culture suits you? What kind of environment does two things for you: 1) gives you a comfortable, peaceful haven; while at the same time 2) provides a catalyst to energize and challenge you? You want a culture, whether it's at home or at work, that does both for you.

Each of us has a different rhythm. Some of us need more excitement, some of us need less. It's time for you to get clear on your environment. We'll start with a broad question on environment, then work on the WHO. Take a brief couple of minute movement break. Just get up and stretch or step outside. As you walk or do something else that gets your blood going, think about the people and places that make you feel alive and complete.

Defining Your Environment

GO

Think about people and places that make you feel alive.

STEPS

1. **Describe the culture** — the kind of place where you like the way things get done around there — that brings out the best in you. Easygoing? Fast paced? Diverse? Familiar?

2. **What (who) else do you want** in your environment that you've dreamt of having?

3. **Complete these sentences:**

    The elements of a great place to live and work include . . .

    My environment will support a mindset of . . .

This is some important insight in the role WHERE will play for you. Remember, WHERE is a physical location that creates your ideal state of mind.

The Who of Life

The people you live and work and play with are dramatically important to your happiness. Let's look at who is in your life right now. Who are the givens in your life? Who do you need to be around? Who encourages you in thinking about what you want to make of your life?

Who's Who: Givens in Your Life. The next activity gets you clear about who are the "Givens" you need by your side. For example, if you have a partner, spouse, best friend you want to move in with — that person becomes a Given. This is someone who is or will be co-located with you physically, mentally or both. We're also going to list people you'll be in contact with, and people you'll work with.

Who Givens: People Who Come along for the Ride

Identify the people who are absolute Givens in your life — they are your traveling companions, no matter what. If you're not married or partnered, or don't have other close family members at your side, the answer to the following questions may be none, or the dream of someone. That's OK. Even if "don't know" is your response, just considering the question is enough. We're getting clear on your situation today.

STEPS

1. **Name the person** or people who will be with you as you find your next *WHAT*.

   Name:

   Role in your life (be descriptive):

2. **Name the people** you will keep In close contact with over the next year—friends, family and colleagues.

   Name:

   Role in your life (be descriptive):

3. **Will maintaining these relationships require travel?**

4. **How do these WHO Givens affect the culture you want** — the way you want to do things in your life?

5. **What would make it worth moving away from your Givens?**

Who's Who: Triggers in Your Life. Who triggers excitement, joy, exploration, adventure and all the things that keep you healthy and hopeful? A good example for me is my husband. While he provides comfort and safety, he can also be one hell of a good Trigger for me. He will push and challenge me, ask tough questions, and give me great feedback. He helps me be more than I was yesterday.

I also continuously look for new Triggers in my life. I like finding people who can egg me on and complement me. So you may have some of those people in your life now, and you want to list them. But you also may be looking for them, in particular as you look at your work environment and your community. What people do you want to work with? Who rounds you out?

Activity 12

WHO Triggers: People Who Nudge You Along

GO

Identify individuals (or kinds of people) you want to keep in your life to continually challenge you, develop you, and support you.

STEPS

1. **Below, identify the people** who are currently your Triggers. This could be the same people in your Given list or new ones.

   Name:

   How they trigger your growth (be descriptive):

2. **Name the kinds of people you want to attract** into your life, work or personal, to help you grow. (This can range from someone to rock climb with to someone you can confide in over coffee.)

   Kind of Person:

   Attributes:

3. **Describe what you need from others** to balance you out.

4. **Where will you find these people? How will you find them?**

5. **How might the people** who are your Givens and Triggers affect your life and career plans?

Note: Triggers may also be people who stir up anxiety and emotion. This is a challenge — so pay attention to it.

Mapping Your WHERE

Now it's time to tie the WHO and WHERE sides together. There are a couple of aspects to it. First, there's the physical part — what town, what country, rural or city, mountains or beach. The second side is the feel of it, the weather, the tone, and the pace of daily life. Keep in mind that the WHERE-WHO are flip sides of the same coin. They're both elements of the environment you're creating. And as Richard Florida's research shows, where you are determines who you will be with.

In order to see the intersection of WHO and WHERE, you're going to put the pieces together on a map. Sean, as you remember, picked Denver on his map. WHERE made a monumental difference in his life. The corporate suit environment "inside the beltway" wore him down. Being a great athlete and an avid outdoorsman, he had the guts to quit his job and take off for Denver, where he could ski, hike and work in an environment less smothering for him than D.C. Once he made the move, he was freed up to concentrate on seeking a satisfying WHAT in his life.

Some of us need a change of address to gain a change of pace. By getting to a place where the tempo and temperament are better suited to us, we get freed up to concentrate on what we love to do. Then, like a trek to find the Sierra Madre treasure, we have more fun working towards the goals we set for ourselves. So let's look at the elements of your map.

Activity 13

WHO and WHERE Map

GO

Diagram and understand where you want to be, where your loved ones are (or want to be), and the impact that will have on your choices.

STEPS

1. **Use the U.S. map and/or world map** (page 73) **for the activity below.** Place a big X on your current location and write "Start" next to it.

2. **Using green for go and yellow for caution, identify areas** of the country (world) where you could see yourself living and working happily in the future. It's where you can bring your WHO and WHERE together, so you can pursue the WHAT that will bring out the best in you. Consider opportunities that could exist in that part of the country (world), such as tech jobs in California's Silicon Valley, research jobs in the pharmaceutical belt of the Northeast, marine biology in Florida or California. And don't forget to consider the personality of the city — whether driven by sun, snow, creativity or history.

3. **Color the area with a bright color** that is the location of your current investigation and place an X there, marking it "End." This is a possibility of your WHERE — the place you expect *Guided Drift* to pull you toward your next opportunity.

4. **Place a check mark** where your loved one(s) is that you want to be with and color that area a different color (if it's with you, simply place a check mark next to your "End" X).

5. **Write about what you discovered** by doing this map. What issues are raised by looking at the combination of your WHO and WHERE? Lifestyle? Fit? Distance? Travel?

6. **What insights** into the role WHO and WHERE play in your life have you gained? What's on the table for you now?

Assembling the Clues from Your Maps

It's time to call out what you love about your WHO and WHERE, and your Givens and Triggers. This is all in the interest of making you more mobile and creative in shaping a life and work environment that works wherever you are. Whether finding your environment means a move across the country, a move in your head, or a simple feng shui redesign of your living space — learning about this now will help you build the knowledge to adapt and find your best fit in this world. This way, you could be OK going anywhere, because you're already in a headspace where you can take your environment with you — whether it's across town or across the globe.

Activity 14

Assembling the WHERE Clues

GO

Look at the Givens and Triggers of WHERE. Answer the questions that apply to you right now. If you're totally satisfied with your WHERE, describe what you love about it and why.

STEPS

1. **Name the Givens** you require for where you want to live and work.

2. **How much of that do you have now?** A little? Half? Most? What's missing, if anything?

3. **Would living in a different environment** right now trigger excitement about exploring your WHAT? How?

   If you're happy with your WHERE, then move ahead. If you are really in need of a where shake-up in your life, I suggest you do that first, then come back and continue work on your WHAT. Consult the *Resource Center* under *WHAT-WHERE-WHO Now?* for more help.

Let's bring all your thoughts in a tighter circle. Reread your responses to Activities 10–14, (in this chapter) and then get some exercise before you answer the summary below. If you need to try something new, remember the *Movement* section of the *Resource Center.*

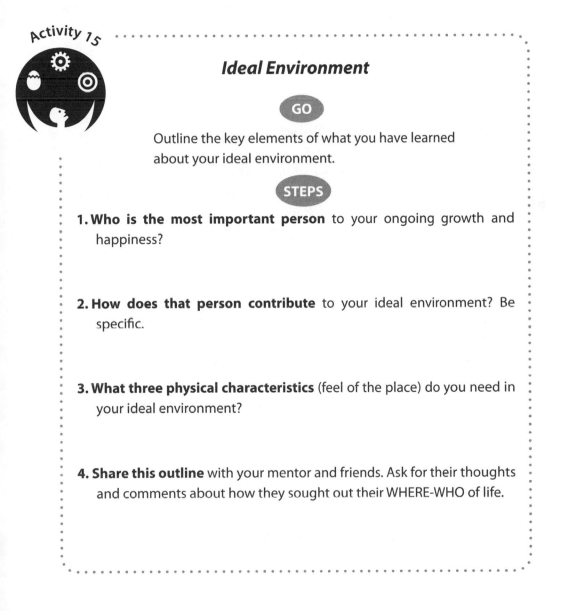

Activity 15

Ideal Environment

GO

Outline the key elements of what you have learned about your ideal environment.

STEPS

1. **Who is the most important person** to your ongoing growth and happiness?

2. **How does that person contribute** to your ideal environment? Be specific.

3. **What three physical characteristics** (feel of the place) do you need in your ideal environment?

4. **Share this outline** with your mentor and friends. Ask for their thoughts and comments about how they sought out their WHERE-WHO of life.

Activity 15, is a placeholder for you. As you work on the WHAT, don't ever let go of the WHERE-WHO side of developing a fulfilling life. Your WHAT is one side of your future. Always keep its place inside the environment you want to create and the way you want to do things around your life. As my friend Steve says, work is not a burden, it is a blessing. And we can enjoy it as a blessing when we have created a well-rounded life. With WHO and WHERE as your backdrop, you're ready to explore your WHAT.

WHAT Exploration

Let's take a progress check here. Up to this point you've taken some time to get clear on the first two of three questions we continually revisit in life — the WHO and WHERE of life. For most of us, these questions are always in play, but they're squeezed under the surface of daily living. Not any more.

Now that you've shed some light on the environment you are creating for yourself, a key part of getting to WHAT is choice-making. You don't wake up one day, after college graduation or some other milestone, to find your boat waiting to help you cross the sea of destiny and take you to the shore of enlightenment. Instead, you find yourself at your personal shoreline, which has been determined by the choices you have made up to that point.

You <u>can</u> take a deliberate and conscious stand on the choices of your life. We tend, however, not to take stands. We often let choices roll over us. But now you have a compass in hand that has fixed two of your three triangulation points — the WHO and WHERE.

Sean is a great example of paying attention at the right time. By focusing on his WHERE first, he totally immersed himself into discovering the WHAT. The interference noise of being unhappy in his first WHERE vanished. Sean needed a WHERE shake-up to clear his head and concentrate on what made him happy, so he could land the next best job for right now.

Looking at Past as Preparation. Every choice you've made has brought you to today. But I don't want you to ignore your past. If you've not been paying enough attention to how you got where you are today, then looking at your past now is perfect timing. We're not going to do a big research project. I want you to scan your past, like you're taking a helicopter ride over your life experiences to date. You'll see things you wouldn't normally see at ground level. In the next activity, you'll take that 10,000-foot aerial ride over your past.

Personal Timeline

Create a timeline of your past, with a few stops at some key points along the way — childhood, teenage years, college/young adult years, and adult (post-twenties, if you've gotten there yet). Treat this as if you're flying in a circle around this territory called your history, and you want to see it from different perspectives.

1. **Prepare for each timeline.** The worksheet for the next activity will ask you three different questions about each timeframe of your life. You may have answers for some, and not for others — it's very individual. Below are some hints on things to think about as you look at the timelines and complete them:

   Timeline 1: What happened to you that you think helped shape the person you are today? Include everything from troubles to terrific high points, from proud moments to the routine of daily living.

   Timeline 2: What did you love to do? What got you psyched up? Whether you loved riding bikes or listening to music, put that down and why. What made you feel great about yourself? This is not about whether you won trophies — it's about what was fun for you — whether it was racing on the summer swim team or reading the *New York Times* every day, watching TV or drawing — somewhere in your past is a seed of your passion.

Timeline 3: The third timeline asks about people that influenced your life. Who pops up on your mental screen as a guide and mentor? Who do you respect and want to be proud of you? Think of family, friends, seasoned professionals, co-workers and bosses.

2. **Turn to page 79** and spend fifteen to thirty minutes completing the timeline.

3. **After completing the worksheet, take a few minutes and answer the following questions.** You will do a further analysis in the next activity, so simply scan the worksheet for now.

   a. What trends and patterns, if any, do you notice across your life?

   b. Is there anything that stands out as a particular passion?

   c. What else is worth paying attention to as you focus on your WHAT?

   d. What ideas here might grow into favorite hobbies or avocations?

Let's face it, the past is part of our future. Each of us needs to see clearly what's in our backpack — what's behind us that we carry with us all our life. The clues are there — they may show up at different times, but there are always dots we can connect.

My friend Matt, who really struggled with remembering anything from childhood, did remember how shy he was, how he lived in the world of books, and how hard it was to make friends. As he talked more about this, he discovered how much reading he does — how he is very up-to-date on international affairs — and indeed reads the *New York Times* from cover to

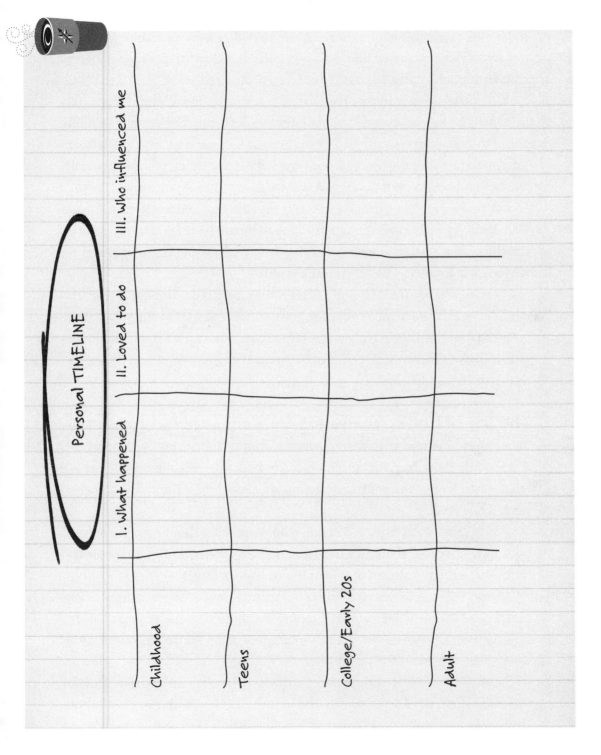

Personal TIMELINE

I. What happened

II. Loved to do

III. Who influenced me

Childhood

Teens

College/Early 20s

Adult

cover every day! This exploration led him to realize how much historical and news research interested him. As a result, he struck off to pursue an internship with public radio, to begin his research career.

Why do we spend time on the past? Because it's the molecules that make up who you are now, and it shapes the choices and the decisions you're going to make next. Good, bad or indifferent — your past is your platform for departure. As long as you keep working on preparing yourself to make choices and act on them, your past only matters as that platform.

Let's take a look at what you wrote in the timeline and work the information. Before you do that, though, it's time to move. I want you to reread your timeline. Just read it. Don't analyze it, don't make super improvements on it — a quick jot, fine, but this is not a rewrite.

As soon as you take it in, pull a fifteen-minute hiatus. Step away from the page and let this seep into your pores, your brain cells, and your gut. You are going to draw on this in a big way. This is foundation stuff that contributes to driving you forward. So go move (remember the *Movement* section of the *Resource Center*). Go do it.

The Joy of Under-analysis.
Before we go any further, I want to talk about the joy of under-analysis. I know it sounds hokey, but it's important. A friend of mine has a message on his e-mail: "If the under-analyzed life isn't worth living, the overanalyzed life isn't much to write home about either." How true.

PAY ATTENTION

Listen

What's your next move?

When I say pay attention, I mean: stop, look and listen to your heart and your gut. Check in, then dive back into some experience. Don't dawdle too long — you might miss an opportunity for *Guided Drift*!

Action teaches us more than kinda/sorta thinkin' about it, or endless pondering. Living often feels like a mountain climb without a compass — try a route, see if it works out, go one more mile, then sit down, reconnoiter, reflect, then try the next possibility.

So as you look at your timeline, if you're going to err on any side, let it be on under-analysis. I want you to find just the right amount of meditation. Human beings learn best by doing. Because when your whole body, mind and soul are in it, you can grasp what's happening to you — even if only your body gets it at first. That's why I ask you to move.

We don't just think with our heads. Your body tells you when it gets stressed out, because you get sore muscles, a headache or a cold. Your body also tells you when you're on a roll. You feel invigorated and you smile more.

In this process we're getting your whole body to participate in the equation. Don't over-analyze it, just let the movement work its way through you. I want to take advantage of how your body talks to you by kicking in every piece of data that's sparking in your body from the tactile, to the gut, to the thinking and the being parts.

One more suggestion: progress over perfection. As we begin to do these different activities that help you think through getting to WHAT, take a bias for action, but without the weight of self-judgment. We sometimes think there is a perfect answer out there.

My clients often remind me: "Perfect is the enemy of the good." If we're looking for perfect it just doesn't come that often. Good is good enough. Don't get yourself hyped up over perfect. My dear friend and mentor in educational research, Homer Coker, wrote once, "First best is too expensive, second best comes too late, third best is good enough." There it is! That's the focus I want you to take. He emphasized experimentation over pondering, bruised knees over doing nothing. So let's go have an under-analysis fest and see what pops out. Lest you worry that "good enough" be under-achieving, remember Edison's quest to invent the light bulb. As the story goes, on the two thousand and first try, he got the filament to work. If he had worked for perfection each time, he would have been incredibly frustrated! Instead, good enough step-by-step led him to know 2,000 ways not to build a light bulb — and what a repertoire of skills he built up.

Research says it takes about 10,000 hours of practice to master a skill — whether it's piano or surgery, baseball or carpentry. And you don't get there by expecting perfection at every turn. This is a "steady as she goes" art form. So let's apply some of it.

Timeline Analysis

Look at the things you love to do. This is the bedrock. If you're not drawing on the energy that came with your unique package of skills and talents, then you're not really developing your WHAT or tapping into your sense of purpose. I want you to root out the passion and energy of who you are and apply it to what you do.

A good example is Lance Armstrong. He tells a great story of how he loved to ride his bike as a kid. He loved it so much it became his work, and he ended up doing it for a living. Impossible? Voila, presto and data proof that people can do it. Yeah, maybe the Lance example isn't the norm, but what if it could be?

"When you follow your bliss . . . doors will open . . ."
– Joseph Campbell

I'm going to give you my all time favorite quote now, from well-known teacher of mythology, Joseph Campbell:

> "If you follow your bliss, you put yourself on a kind of track that has been there all the while, waiting for you, and the life that you ought to be living is the one you are living. When you can see that, you begin to meet people who are in your field of bliss, and they open doors to you. I say, follow your bliss and don't be afraid, and doors will open where you didn't know they were going to be."

The keys to what we love to do begin in our childhood. Let's move into one more layer of the timeline analysis. This is about understanding more deeply what you just wrote, so you can draw on it consistently over time. We're building up some muscle memory here, something you can draw on automatically in a pinch, without going into a tizzy of mass reflection, depression or hyperactivity.

Activity 17

Timeline Analysis

GO

Uncover what story the timeline tells.
Answer the following questions.

STEPS

1. **What story does the "What happened" timeline tell?**

   What clues are there for figuring out your WHAT?

2. **What story does the "Loved to do" timeline tell?**

   What clues are there for figuring out your WHAT?

3. **What story does the "People/Influences" timeline tell?**

   What clues are there for figuring out your WHAT?

4. **How might you translate** childhood or other passions into a career and a calling? For example, if you loved to put on plays as a kid, perhaps you might love sales, teaching, or screenwriting; if you loved to read, maybe you are destined to be a researcher. Or if, like Lance Armstrong, you loved to ride your bike, you're just going to keep doing what you loved from the very beginning!

5. **What else is coming up** for you after reviewing your timeline?

6. **Reread what you wrote** and highlight anything that stands out for you, including reinforcing your WHO and WHERE, and identifying your WHAT.

Brewing and Stewing. You've just gotten a handle on your past. Things are brewing for you. If you're not seeing it, and you're feeling like you are stewing in your own juices, then read to the end of this section and stop. Hit the *Movement* part of the *Resource Center,* do some kind of movement, work the timeline questions again.

Are you grabbing on too hard? This is not the time to push against your instincts. *Some* stewing is OK. Sometimes the best stuff comes out of marinating in the juices — in this case the combined juices of your instincts and your abilities. But you will burn out if you don't get moving again.

This is fish or cut bait time. The only way you're going to make it in the next set of activities is to know where you're coming from and to pull out of hiding. Your door is out there.

You're on the cusp of getting to your *WHAT*. Before you get too excited about unveiling the wizard behind the curtain, take this in. I want you to stay excited, but I don't want you to think that the next part of your *WHAT* is the be all and end all. *WHAT* evolves over life. So let's look at another way to ask the question.

Always Be Willing to Play the Opposite. We've just been working step-by-step, and now it's time to do just the opposite. I'm going to take a crack at the big questions. You've done a little thinking, you've done a little walking, and you've done a little analysis. You probably have more answers than you think, especially after thinking about your past. If you don't feel your timeline has kick-started things for you, now is the time to go back to that exercise and consult a friend or mentor.

If you're ready to move on, then you're ready to think big for a moment. If you can't answer the question in the next activity right now, don't worry. But I advise you to think from your gut. Your gut and your heart are far quicker in figuring things out than your head. I know you've had an experience with thinking, "I should have listened to my gut." It's all part of listening to your body's natural response system. So I don't care how high flying, how wild and out there your response is, just put whatever comes to your mind in the box for the next question. It's a clue.

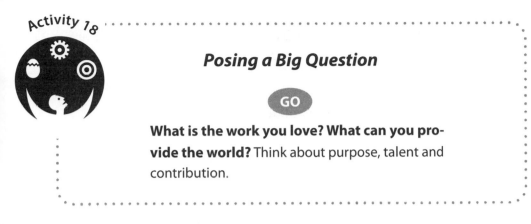

Activity 18

Posing a Big Question

GO

What is the work you love? What can you provide the world? Think about purpose, talent and contribution.

You may have just stumbled across one more clue. Talking about clues, let's go back to that Sierra Madre treasure. I really like thinking about what you're doing as a treasure hunt. Step back and think, "How else could I look at this? How would my mentor, favorite teacher, best friend think about this? What could my next step be to find out more?" Say these questions out loud and then answer them out loud.

Tip: Read Your Responses Out Loud

If you haven't started doing it by now — stand up and start reading your responses out loud to yourself. This is your first way of seeing how it fits — like trying on a pair of jeans. You can't know by just looking — you have to get your body into it.

This also serves you as a step towards committing yourself to action. Say it out loud to yourself and you can say it out loud to someone else. It's rehearsal. Something magical happens when I ask the question out loud. Even what seemed dumb or too simple takes on new shape.

I try to never forget that simple is profound. The simplest stuff is usually the hardest to answer. That question you just took a crack at — your purpose and contribution — is a pretty simple question with a lot of punch.

If you need to backtrack and re-think the timeline, and the big question, do it now.

Stepping-stones from Past to Present

In the interest of building the classic map to the treasure, we're taking some stepping-stones from past to present in our next exercise. Take a look at what's going on in your world right now and what's driving you.

A word on doing these next activities, though. When you do this kind of work, you're happily creating a mini nervous breakdown — not the kind where you go nuts, but the kind where you purposefully try to break down barriers.

Don't get freaked out here. Not only is this OK, but it is desirable. The only way we change is to actually break apart the way our brain neurons fire right now — how we're wired to keep doing the things we have been doing. By doing this thinking, moving and creating we stimulate our old neural pathways to un-attach from where they've been connected and reattach to our new targets.

It's unplugging from what isn't working, and plugging into what will work better. It's just like learning to climb that mountain more efficiently, so it's more fun. If I want to get better at climbing, I've got to redirect how those muscle fibers fire in order for my leg and arm muscles to strengthen and reshape themselves — lots of lunges and push-ups.

My friend Rachael did exactly this. She made the bold decision to move from Philadelphia to San Francisco with very little safety net. Why? She needed to break from a longtime relationship and she needed a rich diversity of opportunities and people to be around. In short, she needed to break away and begin again. Was she scared? Was she worried about money? Absolutely. And she took the leap anyway. As good old Yoda says, "Try? There is no try. There is only do or not do."

Same thing applies to figuring out your WHAT and breaking old patterns and habits. So go ahead and have a little nervous breakdown on me.

Activity 19

Breaking from the Past

Identify the stepping-stones that will pull you from past to present to future.

Stone 1: Bridge from past to present

Reread your timeline if you need some grounding. Considering everything that's on there, what are you proudest of accomplishing? What called out to you, like something you were compelled to do?

Write it down and tell a little story about it.

Stone 2: Dealing with you right here, right now

What's going on right now that you have to deal with before you can move on? I want to see every roadblock, every "omigod," every "Oh, but . . ." on here: "I'm afraid to try, I don't have enough money, my parents/family don't agree, I'm afraid to move, I've got commitments, I've got habits that are hard to break"—whatever, put it down here.

Stone 3: What are your instincts and itches to change?

Bring It In. You just captured on one page the energy from your past, all the stuff that is swirling for you right now, and the magnets that are pulling you forward. These are the stepping-stones to your future.

Heads Up. There is one more thing to complete before you go back to your mentor for a conversation. You have looked at the past and the present, now let's look ahead and visualize the kinds of things you would love to be doing.

5

Shaping Your Futures

Yes, I said futures in the plural. As we move into the last exercise of getting to WHAT, before you get some input from your mentor, I want you to get hold of this idea of plural futures.

Zeroing in on Your WHAT

Most of us grow up thinking there is "A" future for us — the one that appears in neon flashing lights on the big billboard. Not true! Not true! Not true! Each of us has many futures. As such, I want you to keep a foot firmly in a commitment to a next step . . . AND . . . open to whatever possibilities may present themselves — creating the opportunity for *Guided Drift*. It is important to consider all the parts of who you are as you narrow down a WHAT arena. Consider who you are at school, at work, in your hobbies, in your family, and in your community work.

Take my friend Steve. He is truly a sunny, good-humored, kind man. These attributes led him to a job in sales, which ultimately led to a marketing executive position. At mid-life he reassessed the kind of impact he wanted to have on the world — including spending more time with his kids (you travel *a lot* when you're a marketing exec). His friendliness, his caring, and his passion for learning led him to become a fifth-grade teacher. A slight (hah!) cut in pay, yes, but the rewards through impact on young lives—astounding. And lo and behold, he got invited to teach at the college where he did his master's degree in education during the summer months. Then, five years later he was asked to guide the future of the program as the director of graduate studies in education—now applying his love of learning and his strategic marketing skills to build a strong program supporting the local schools. Connected dots indeed.

I also want to minimize confusion as much as I can. I want you to make choices, so you can narrow down your area of concentration and get results. But just because you made a choice, it doesn't mean you're locked into that forever. My first boss, my lifelong best boss, Wray Stout, said to my husband and me many years ago when we made a decision to move cross-country: "You make the decision, then you make the decision right." He meant that just because you make a decision doesn't mean you can't change it when you get more information later on.

Making the decision, though, allows you to move forward, and to learn something. Sometimes, as in our cross-country move, we ended up back where we started. That's OK! Because then we knew, right down to our bones, what was the best thing for us. We literally moved our bodies and our lives, to find out what fit us.

Incremental, step-by-step choices actually allow you to make more informed choices as you go along. It's being willing to start that dot collection without being totally sure how they'll connect—concrete clues about what you love and what you need to be happy. Those clues have information about many different parts of your futures. You have the play side, the hobby side, the friends side, the sports side, the music side, the loaf on the couch and watch football (or chick-flick) side, the career side, the studious side, the feeling side, the thinking side, the partying side, the expert side—the list could go on and on. The more you know about all of them, the more you can get them to play together instead of ignore each other. Like a diamond, in poor light it's just another rock—but when you pull it into the light, all the facets can shine.

Dreaming about Your Futures

Let's get that stuff to play together. We're going to do that by dreaming. Don't worry, I'm not going to take you to la-la land and leave you there. We're going to look at the picture buried in your head of what else is possible for you and bring it into better focus.

We are not human unless we're dreaming. If we don't have dreams, then our futures are lifeless. They grab hold of us and put us on a hyperlink into the future. They also are part of what helps us make decisions. If you're not seeing a future that pulls out the best in you, then what does?

In the next activity I want you to let the floodgates open again. This is a record of all the "gee, I wish I . . . woulda, coulda, wanna, what ifs . . ." that are floating around in your life.

Activity 20

Dream Your Futures

GO

Look out five years and visualize what you could be doing. It doesn't matter how vague your picture of the future is — whether it's technical, artistic, talking, or teaching — you can see someplace where you are working.

STEPS

1. **Imagine putting a disc into your forehead**, and playing the video of your future. As the story rolls, notice what you are doing, what people around you are doing, where you are, and the spirit and energy of the work situation. Don't worry if you can't see the name of the organization — but see you at your best work, having fun, contributing to the planet. On a team? By yourself? Outside? Inside? Busy? Calm? Managing people or managing projects? Thinking or doing?

2. **Close your eyes now, and roll the tape.** Do this in a quiet place where you won't feel weird closing your eyes and imagining.

   NOTE: If negative or limiting images creep in, stop the process and take a movement break. Set the intention before you move to focus on past experiences of confidence, contribution and fun. What does your past timeline say about these kinds of things? Do something especially fun when you move — like dancing or a favorite sport. Get silly, laugh, get rowdy. Let this energy release create a calmness that will give you the space to focus on doing great things.

3. **Jot down all the things you saw** when you looked into the future — your video.

4. **How do you feel about what you saw?**

Nothing is more powerful than a vivid dream. Even though dreams are fuzzy and disjointed, they feed us and draw us to achieve our potential. Once you have a dream, as Martin Luther King said, then you go ahead and climb the next step — even though you can't see the staircase. It will appear. So let's draw on these dreams of yours.

Activity 21

Taking the Next Step with Your Coffee House Blueprint

GO

Pull together your ideas from your past, present and futures dream activities.

STEPS

1. **What possibilities** from your dreams list seem realizable to you?

2. **Compare the ideas that have emerged** to your original *Coffee House Blueprint*. List up to five areas, including one or all on your original *Blueprint* (page 21).

   1.

   2.

   3.

   4.

   5.

3. **Now that you have some futures identified,** how does each one make you stretch?

4. **What examples do you see** in the real world that you want to find out more about?

5. **Which three are pulling the hardest? Why?**

   1.

   2.

   3.

Focus on the Here and Now

Now that you've dreamed about your futures, we're going to bring it into the present. There is nothing stronger than the power of the present moment. My friend, Barry Oshry, who has spent his lifetime teaching people about their own power and tapping into the power of their team, used to tell a story about the actress Katharine Hepburn, a star of the big Hollywood productions era in the mid twentieth century. Before she was well known, a reporter interviewed her at a coffee shop. When he asked her what she did, she said definitively, "I'm a movie star." He told her that few people knew who she was, and she was not a bit worried or resentful, continuing to tell him that she was indeed a movie star. She put herself in the moment of stardom. It was the certainty and confidence that made all the difference. So below, state what difference you will make — what your "starring role" is.

Activity 22

Your Declaration

Write your own "Katharine Hepburn"-style declaration. This is your present statement. This is your stand. There will be no wishy-washy words like "I'll try, I wish, I will be, I want to be." Put your statement down as if your dream is your reality. "I am . . . , I write . . . , I construct . . . ," etc. Throw some adverbs in there to describe how you work (creatively, energetically, etc.) Check out *Power up Your Elevator Pitch* in the *Resource Center* to get a list of verbs and adjectives that could help you. Get a clear picture of your target and describe it in detail.

DECLARATION:

_____

Why Write a Declaration. The approach here is not to narrow your life down to a tiny pathway, but to make choices that let you enjoy to the fullest what you have chosen. You may not meet the exact ideal you've created because new things take precedence. You could end up making choices that carry you to a byway, and that's OK. If you DO know where you're going, and you need to adjust because priorities or desires change, at least you still have your bearings (oh yes, there it is again, *Guided Drift*).

Ideal is about hanging that star out there, it's not about "Omigod, I'm going to disappoint myself if I don't do exactly what I set out to do." I walked a marathon a couple of years ago. I had an ideal of wanting to walk about a fourteen-minute mile and finishing in under six hours. I didn't make it, I finished in about six and a half hours, but it didn't matter. The nugget of the ideal was to have the experience of the marathon, to train, to enjoy the people, and to finish. Things change! I had other things to do, and I gave it all I had at that point. I did damn good! I was proud to have done it, better than not to have tried at all.

So as you work with this ideal statement, it's not that you're saying to the people mentoring you or talking to you about career opportunities, that you have to have this tomorrow. It's that you see yourself engaging in work that draws on these skills and talents. One thing leads to another, and you'll likely find yourself in a job that is not an exact match to what you predicted, but has core elements to keep you happy and growing.

The Power of a Pitch

When I had my own new beginning writing this book I had to walk around a park and say this kind of stuff out loud. I was developing a new identity for myself. By placing myself in the role, it became more real for me. I used to think, oh, they're going to think I'm conceited for saying I'm writing a book — and they'll ask me how it's going! But the more I said it, the more I committed to some self-talk that this is really what I'm all about. And it helped me become it. Of course, it's a good thing that people ask me how the books and programs are coming—it provides guidance and incentive to keep going!

Announcing your intentions to the world puts your *Guided Drift* into play. You are building a snappy, quick statement that you can use on everyone from the person you meet in a coffee shop, to someone interviewing you. In the marketing business they call this your "elevator pitch." If you had thirty seconds in an elevator with a potential customer (you can think interviewer), can you get them interested? You're looking for a response like, "Gee, interesting, tell me more!"

Use your declaration as the cornerstone for your pitch. Read it out loud. Once you've done that, I want you to stand, move away from your desk, and take a walk. This time you do need to take a walk, because as you walk you're going to actually do a rehearsal of what you just wrote. It doesn't have to be in the exact same words, and in fact you don't want it to be.

By now you should be up, you have the book in hand and you're walking. Complete the following activity. Go ahead, practice, say it out loud, pitch it three or four different ways. It's OK to take a few minutes and really get into it.

Activity 23

Building Your Elevator Pitch

GO

Make your dreams more concrete by rehearsing their descriptions and condensing them into your pitch. (If the term pitch sounds too "salesy" to you, think of it in baseball terms—if you don't pitch, there is no game.)

STEPS

1. Re-read your Declaration to get your footing for this pitch.

2. **Answer the following questions:**

   a. What will you provide to the world?
   b. What do you want to be known for? What can you promise?
   c. Who will you serve?
   d. What passions are you satisfying?
   e. What beliefs do you have that will impact your work?
   f. What values drive you?

3. **Craft a statement of twenty-five words or less** that includes all the elements above.

4. **Now capture your unique proposition** to the world in three to ten words. You may have to come back to this over several weeks. I find it evolves as you get clearer about what you do. As of today, mine is "Bringing your talent to life." Yes, it can be done. Think of Nike — "Just do it."

   Consult the *Resource Center* section *Power up Your Elevator Pitch*, and of course, the thesaurus, for help with verbs and adjectives.

5. **Say your pitch out loud,** in several different ways. It might even be nice to record it (I use the recording gizmo on my iPod). Or just stand in front of the bathroom mirror and talk to yourself. If this feels like too much, close your eyes and run the mind's-eye tape, seeing yourself saying it out loud. Every step gets you closer to the real thing — talking about your aspirations with others.

6. **Now imagine** that someone just stopped you in the park, tapped you on the shoulder, and asked you what you do? Practice telling them, using the key words from your pitch. Record it if possible.

7. **Thoughts?**

Now that you've said it out loud, and rehearsed the presentation, we're going to get ready to have a conversation with your mentor.

Connecting with Your Mentor

Let's get clear on what these mentoring sessions are. They are NOT about getting great concurrence with what you have created. You're not asking for a YES man to say "Oh, you're wonderful, good job, I like what you've done." The whole point of this is to stir things up for you. As you get feedback, look for the differences from your point of view. Listen up! This is so important — the mentor is there to support you, or he wouldn't give you the incredible gift of his time. Your job is to probe.

Tips for Being a "Mentee"

1. Facilitate the conversation and ask open-ended questions. Point him to your summary documents, then get his input. What do you think of my progress so far? What stands out for you? How do you see this lining up with what you know about me?

2. Share some of your research and your thinking.

3. Listen hard — to his words, but much more — his face, his body movements. He may try to be "nice" in the beginning, but his body will give him away. You may pick up a signal from his eyes that tells you this is just the tip of the iceberg. Dig. Go ahead and ask: "What did you really mean?" "Can you give me an example?" "Give it to me straight."

4. Take notes. This is tricky — because I do want you to watch his face and reactions. But you won't remember everything if you don't take notes. Ask him to take notes too to help you out — or to draw and sketch things out.

With these tips in mind you're ready to have a substantial conversation with your mentor. You are, of course, checking in with him as you need to, but now you have a lot of ideas to discuss. So take some time to prep for it.

Preparing for Mentor Meeting

Prepare your mentor for the upcoming coaching session. The focus of this meeting is to talk about your discoveries, to take a time-out with your mentor and get some feedback for your next moves.

1. **Call her**, this is personal — please don't e-mail.

   Sample conversation (as always, make this your own): *"Hey Jodi, I've done a little prep work, I'd like to sit down and talk with you about it. I have a set of questions that I want to ask you (see Tips for Mentees on the previous page), and then I'd like to find about an hour, if possible, and get your input into some of the things I've been working on. I'm going to send you an e-mail with the work I've prepared up to now, and also with the questions I'll be asking you. If you want, I can send you some ideas about mentoring from the program I'm working with. It might help us with our conversation."* (You'll find the Tips for Mentors after this activity.)

2. **Send her an e-mail** that says: *"Hi Jodi, Thanks so much for agreeing to meet on X date, X time and X place (be sure to confirm in your e-mail). I'm really happy to be meeting you at X Coffee House. Please find below a summary of what I see myself doing in the future. I thought this would help by giving you some background for our meeting."*

3. **Your summary** can include your *Pitch,* your mental video of the future, items from your timeline, such as what you loved to do, what you know about how you get in your own way, and anything else you think might help. Stay brief, one or two short paragraphs, or six to eight bullet points.

4. **Send a second e-mail** two to three days before you meet, just to confirm your meeting.

   "Thanks a lot, looking forward to next (Thursday, May 4th). I'll see you at X location, X time."

5. **Review the *"Mentee" Tips*** above an hour before you arrive.

6. **Arrive early**, with notebook in hand. Prepare yourself for an exciting conversation.

7. **Focus your discussion** on what is most important to you now, doubts and concerns you have, suggestions your mentor has for you. Plan some questions, but also let it unfold however it goes. Sometimes the best insights come from what isn't on the agenda.

8. **Hand write a thank you note** and send it within twenty-four hours. If you can't bring yourself to do this, absolutely write an e-mail thank you — but I sure do prefer the idea of a hand-written note!

Tips for Mentors

1. Ask encouraging questions to get your "mentee" to talk about his interests.

2. Look for indicators that he is passionate about the areas he is pursuing. Does he get excited when he talks about it? Does his face light up? Feel free to ask direct questions: What do you love about this work? Would you do it even if you couldn't get paid for it? Why do you think this is it?

3. Get your "mentee" to give examples of why he thinks this is a good fit. How does it line up with past things he loved to do? How does it line up with what he's good at doing?

4. Tap into your own instincts and be blunt with him — he needs your honest opinion.

What to Do with Input from Mentors. Once you have your input written down and you have the notes from your mentor, read all of the notes and then go do some physical activity. This one should be at the top of your vigorous list — a hearty game of basketball or if you're a dancer go for the tango, or take an even brisker walk. Really, really sweat this one out. Plant what you've read in the back of your mind and go get active to work it into your whole being.

The next thing I want you to do is to work this good feedback right into your gut, so your brain can act on it. Put together what you heard and identify what you will start focusing on. You've made some statements and you've made some choices on the WHO and WHERE, and you've pinpointed that down. Now, we're going to choose your WHAT arena.

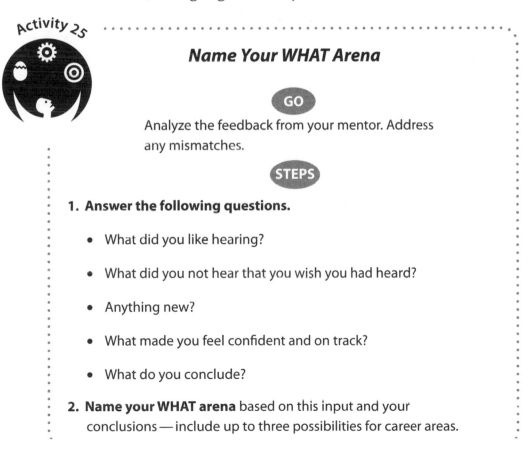

Activity 25

Name Your WHAT Arena

GO

Analyze the feedback from your mentor. Address any mismatches.

STEPS

1. **Answer the following questions.**

   - What did you like hearing?

   - What did you not hear that you wish you had heard?

   - Anything new?

   - What made you feel confident and on track?

   - What do you conclude?

2. **Name your WHAT arena** based on this input and your conclusions — include up to three possibilities for career areas.

1.

2.

3.

3. **Review your original *Coffee House Blueprint*** and make sure it has the date you started this process. Don't get rid of this — it's a good piece of history on your thinking and your original instincts.

4. **Recreate the *Coffee House Blueprint***, put today's date on it. Using the discoveries you made as you created a past timeline, and worked into possible futures, update your *Coffee House Blueprint* with your three key WHAT ideas identified in Step 2 above, and who you might talk to about them, in addition to your mentor. Even if the WHAT areas are the same, the way you write about it may be different — so indulge the process of rewriting — you may uncover a fresh clue!

5. **Add what you know about your WHERE and WHO** to your blueprint.

6. **Place your original and redesigned *Coffee House Blueprint*** in the front of your notebook next to your Contact List and your Project Plan. Refer to these sheets often — they represent your own personal *Guided Drift* plan. I will bet that twenty years from now, when you connect your dots, the trail will lead back here.

Get Set for Reaching Out

If you haven't done much of it yet, it's time to start talking to parents, best friends, a favorite aunt or uncle—the kinds of people you trust. This is a much less formal process than working with your mentor—we'll go back to her shortly for a check-in.

Chat it up and keep thinking it through. As you talk to people, work on getting more specific about the kinds of things you're doing to create opportunity in your WHAT arena. You're backing into your plan. You've got the end game in mind, and you're starting to think about the stepping-stones to get there. The following activity puts you in the head-set of concentrating on what you can do now to coax your desired future to unfold.

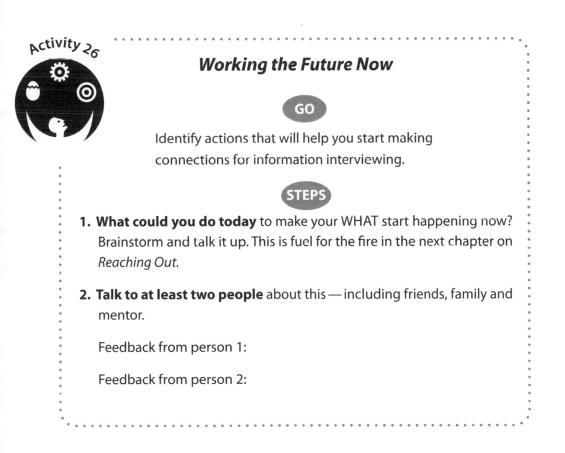

Activity 26

Working the Future Now

GO

Identify actions that will help you start making connections for information interviewing.

STEPS

1. **What could you do today** to make your WHAT start happening now? Brainstorm and talk it up. This is fuel for the fire in the next chapter on *Reaching Out*.

2. **Talk to at least two people** about this—including friends, family and mentor.

   Feedback from person 1:

   Feedback from person 2:

Claim Your Path

You're at a great crossing point now. You have a name for your area of focus. If you're still a little fuzzy about what to call it, consult *Picture Work You Love* in the *Resource Center*. But don't feel you need a required kind of name for this, you may create your own!

I also don't want you to think you have to know what industry or profession you will be in. If you love numbers, you can do financial work in the movie industry, the aviation industry, the toy industry or the non-profit sector. You MAY have a preference, but it's not necessary. Be clear on the type of work you want to do, and don't worry about the industry or type of company you will end up in. That will take care of itself, especially since you have already done your WHO and WHERE homework.

All of us can do many things. And we've probably all done jobs that are in our reach, but not our sweet spot. And how do we know that sweet spot? When time slides past you, it's hard to stop, and you feel like you're making a difference.

Back to the Mentor. You've named your arena(s), you've written down the things you can contribute. Call your mentor—use the next activity to organize the conversation. This is not a long sit down. Send him an e-mail; tell him what you have come up with.

Activity 27

Confirming the WHAT

Get feedback from your mentor on your WHAT-WHERE-WHO and begin building referrals for information interviews.

1. **Open the conversation** (in your own way) something like this: *"I have decided this is what's next for me. I've listened to your feedback, and looked at what I love to do. I realize that by concentrating on this area, I'll be able to contribute best and be happy in my work. Do you have about fifteen minutes to talk now? If not, can we set something up in the next few days?"*

2. **Describe where you are.**

3. **Ask:**

   1. What do you think about where I've landed? Take notes:

   2. What do you know about places to learn more about this area — companies, jobs, work environments? Have a fifteen minute conversation. Take notes:

   3. Do you know anyone I can call and get an information interview with? (This is a starting place for the connections you will be making in the next chapter.)

One more thing. Before you start connecting for information interviews, let's do a check on any roadblocks you're experiencing now.

Tackling Your Roadblocks

GO

Identify what things may hold you back now — both internal and external. You may want to consult your initial thoughts in Activity 2, page 16).

STEPS

1. **Answer the following questions**:

   • As you know you, what are the kinds of things that will hold you back?

   • Identify one thing that is "Outside" — demands the external world puts on you (like finances or getting training).

   • Identify one thing that is "Inside" — What you know about you. Are you afraid of success? Do you struggle with self-confidence? Do you get depressed easily? Are you scattered and unfocused? What one thing will you need support from your mentors and friends on?

2. **How can your mentor or others (list them) help you** with this? This includes getting creative ideas on dealing with financial constraints.

3. **Chat up your *Elevator Pitch*** (from Activity 23, page 96) with friends, family and mentor. Include what you know about your inside and outside roadblocks.

Bring It In. Well, well, well. You've come a long way from where you started. You've now got a path of choice; you've identified what you want to do next, you've taken your stand. We're going to dig in. What you did here was start out with broad ideas on your past, and worked from an ideal future down to what's next, something you can take action on.

Heads Up. You've named your WHAT area(s) and know what kind of WHERE and WHO you need. Now we're going to put your action plan into high gear. This is not classic job hunting and career management stuff. Instead, you're going out there to make something happen by taking advantage of *Guided Drift*. This means it's connection and relationship building time. In the next chapter you will gain skills and confidence in creating groundbreaking conversations.

You have the duty to yourself to both guide and drift. You're cheating yourself if you stick to the super-structured job hunt thing where you scroll through the Internet day after day, send out letters, endlessly perfect your resume, and wait for the right thing to pop up. You're the guidance system—be intentional! That's why I keep talking about paying attention. If you're paying attention, then the right stuff happens on purpose. So get ready, we're moving into action through information interviews, job interviews, and trying out work opportunities in creative ways.

PAY ATTENTION

Guide and Drift

What's your next move?

Reaching Out

You have laid a foundation on which you can build a lifetime of transitions and achievements. Like a tennis player that serves a ball on the sweet spot of the racket, you can't help but ace your serve.

You've put in a lot of work — nice job! You've got your ideal and your WHAT-WHERE-WHO arena(s) identified. You've got feedback from your mentor, you've got a path chosen.

Making Sure Your Plan is SMART

Now it's time to put your plan to work, and make sure you're working smart, not hard. First, though, let's get all the parts working together. Turn the page to the next activity to make headway on that.

Activity 29

An Organizer for Connecting and Networking

GO

Assemble the planning and tracking documents that will assist you in the networking process.

STEPS

1. **Make sure your original and revised *Coffee House Blueprint* are in the** front of your notebook (Activities 3 and 25, pages 21 and 101).

2. **Pull out your original Project Plan** (Activity 8A, page 44) and update it with any new information you have, including goals, deadlines, and resources.

3. **Review your Tool Kit Assembly list** (Activity 4, page 24) to make sure you have everything you need at your fingertips to network.

4. **Find your Contact List** (Activity 8B, page 46) and put it in front of your *Coffee House Blueprint* in the notebook. This is sacred to the next part of this process. Keep track of who you are talking to and when/how you follow up. This will make you golden as a person of your word.

5. **What else do you need to feel organized?** Add it to your notebook.

I have one more thing to add to your notebook before you continue networking. A clever tip I picked up years ago about project planning is to make sure that your goals are SMART: Specific, Measurable, Achievable, Results-oriented, and Time-bound. This is a check on what you put in your Project Plan — and a way to keep you on track. It also asks you to look through your analysis of the 3Ws to note what's important to you. You can tuck this in your notebook with your Project Plan, and I suggest you pull it out when you start getting close to finding the right opportunity.

Activity 30

SMART Check of Your Project Plan

GO

Critique the strength of your Project Plan. You will answer one or two questions in each of the SMART categories. You will be able to answer some of these questions now, and others you will answer when the opportunity arrives.

STEPS

1. **Specific:**

   - Is your WHAT-WHERE-WHO goal clear enough? Will you know it when you see it?

   - How are you working on a good, rather than perfect, next opportunity?

2. **Measurable:**

   - Name your criteria for a good WHAT-WHERE-WHO fit.

   - How well does your opportunity match your criteria?

   - Does it feel like a good fit?

3. **Achievable:**

   - Are you aiming for the job you can get?

   - What makes it achievable?

4. **Results-oriented:**

   - Describe what you're doing to get to the right next opportunity. In particular, are you out there making connections with lots of different kinds of people in your WHAT arena?

   - What do you need to do more of/less of to be results-oriented?

5. **Time-bound:**

   - Are you reviewing your progress on a regular basis with your mentor?

   - How can you improve the discipline of the process?

   - What deadlines do you need (dates by which you will either take a temp job, or use a fallback opportunity)?

These SMART checks are a way to keep you on track and honest with yourself. Use them as a boost when things are getting fuzzy for you. Keep it handy for when you need a check-in with yourself.

Your Ultimate Information Interview Guide

Warming Up. Let's put your plan in high gear. You have already conducted several informal information interviews. You've talked with your mentor and you've interviewed a family member. Now it's time to take the show on the road. This can be the hardest part of the process to warm up to. Sometimes we need help putting ourselves out there, so a little discipline goes far.

Simplicity at Work: Small Steps, Good Questions. If we want to make progress, it's not going to happen by asking big, heavy questions, but rather from many small questions, answers and steps. A good question is one that is both important to you and one you can find an answer to. It moves you a step ahead in your game. Sounds simple, but it's not always easy to do. Here's a personal example.

I aspire to be an accomplished pianist. I played as a kid and had been saying to myself for years that I wanted to get back into it. Finally, I got moving, with a series of questions in my head.

I'm going to walk you through my questions, answers, and actions. Then I'll lead you through your process and help you build a very concrete action plan to make your first connection.

My first question was: how badly do I want to get back to playing piano again? First answer: badly enough to investigate finding a teacher. That led to the next question: "Who do I know that could help me find a teacher?"

Notice — my first thought was on a personal connection, not on a Web site. *This is important!* You want to be nose to nose, making the connection personal. It's much different from e-mail, Internet, or texting.

I remembered that I had served on a committee several years ago with a local symphony member, someone who knew the music scene in my town.

112

So I called her. We reconnected, talked about what we had been doing, and she was more than happy to help. She even checked with the piano teacher to see if she was taking new students before she suggested the right person for me. Her responsiveness shows just how willing people are to help.

Then my internal dialogue continued. "Someone went to a little trouble to find me just the right name." I didn't want to feel like an idiot for asking and not following through. I called the teacher quickly, before I lost the impetus. Calling was a great "ta-da!"—a small win that started some momentum. Like stepping onto a moving escalator, once you take the first step, momentum escorts you to the next level.

Once I met her—because the connection I used knew me well enough to match me up well—the teacher and I just clicked. The next question became: can I fit this into an already busy schedule? So I started by taking a lesson every other week. Later, I moved to weekly lessons and invested in my lifelong dream of purchasing a grand piano. Now I'm fully invested—financially and with my commitment and passion for music.

By posing questions, and letting one lead to the next, you build your momentum. So let's apply this process to getting you connected to people who can help you.

Asking Your Own Guiding Questions

Guideline 1: Is the first question small enough that you're willing to take the step? (For me, calling my orchestra friend for a referral.)

Guideline 2: Does the question get you someplace beyond where you were a moment ago—no matter how small? (Now I had a teacher's name—the resource I needed to proceed.)

Guideline 3: Does the question guide you to DO something that you are passionate about? When we're talking about shaping your 3Ws, does it drive you to act?

Guideline 4: Does each question up the ante? If you're serious about moving ahead, each question should move you closer to making a choice.

The next activity asks you to apply the questions to your own goals. Pay attention to how you're feeling when you're asking and acting on these questions. Are you feeling energized or plodding? If you're plodding, take bigger steps. If you're anxious, take smaller ones.

Activity 31

Warm-up Steps for Information Interviews

GO

Move ahead using small steps to get information interviews and other contacts and connections.

STEPS

1. Ask yourself

Question 1: How badly do I want to find the right match for right now?
Answer 1: Enough to take this next step in getting an information interview about my field of interest:

Question 2: Who could help me find the right people to talk to?
Answer 2: Name one person you will actually connect with:

Question 3: How committed am I to taking the next step?
Answer 3: I'm going to call (visit, e-mail) this person by (date), and follow up every week until I get a response:

Question 4: Am I succeeding in making the time to call (visit, e-mail)? Why? Why not? What else can I do?
Answer 4: Yes, I'm invested enough to (persist with this person, find another person, etc.):

2. Note here what is easy for you, hard for you, where you might need help, and whether you need bigger steps or smaller ones.

The Heart of *Great* Information Interviews

We've been talking for a while about how important information interviews are and you've been gradually building skills in doing them. There are a couple of secrets to remember about great information interviewing. First, this is about creating groundbreaking conversations to get you information. ***It's not a job interview.*** You're not strutting your stuff here, or marketing your abilities. Instead, you're asking questions to gain insight and understanding. The key is to respect the expertise of this person by honoring them with questions that deepen your knowledge and appreciation of their interests, experience, and skills. Your goal is to sow the seeds for great dialogue.

Second, most people want to help—you can create opportunity for the asking. Occasionally, you will run into someone who is just too busy for you. But most of us seasoned performers are flattered when you ask us for help. Flattery does indeed get you somewhere! But it can't be empty and self-serving. Authenticity plays a part here again. Your passion in learning about areas that interest me, as a targeted seasoned performer, will show up in how you ask, how you follow up, and how you interview me.

This is real connection. Once you have made that connection with me, and keep me in the loop, I will want to continue to help you. And there are many more like me out there. Most seasoned performers enjoy teaching and creating a positive influence in the world. All you have to do is gain the courage to ask, and you can gather up all this help with a butterfly net!

Great information interviewing is built by learning how to tap into the wealth of knowledge and experience. We're going to learn a little more about the key role seasoned performers play in your development and getting you the right opportunity for right now.

The Importance of a Seasoned Performer

As you have seen, the imaginations of human beings play a big role in unfolding the next WHAT of our lives. But as we look into our future and visualize the fun and success we will have, we often underestimate the annoying, difficult, or routine aspects of a given line of work. This is why it is so important to learn from people who have been there before us.

Daniel Gilbert, a Harvard psychology professor and author of *Stumbling on Happiness,* explained these kinds of conversations. He showed in his research that our imaginations are weak in creating a real understanding of a career. We can do far better by having an in-depth conversation with an experienced person. It turns out that our similarities far outweigh our differences with any individual we might choose to discuss our careers.

As Gilbert describes it, we would be better off picking any person in a crowd to predict a particular job experience, rather than relying on our imaginations. Because, in the end, this person has actually handled the job requirements, the stress, joy, boredom, excitement, learning and routine. Gilbert calls these people "surrogators"—they've lived the experience for you—and their knowledge is far more dependable than anything you can cook up, based on TV, novels, or idealistic hunches.

Take advantage! Let your seasoned performer serve as your substitute, or your surrogate, as Gilbert describes. Seasoned performer interviews are the ultimate in information interviewing. They give you a taste of what this job is like and give you a glimpse into seeing yourself doing it. While you might want to make excuses about the differences between your seasoned performer and you (like they're from a different generation, they're the opposite gender, they worked in a different part of the country) focus instead on the similarities. This seasoned performer, like you, had aspirations they believed their calling could answer. In fact, you can give a gift to your seasoned performer by giving him time to elaborate on what is exciting about this line of work—perhaps rekindling the passion that started it all!

> "...the best way to predict our feelings tomorrow is to see how others are feeling today."
> *–Daniel Gilbert*

Benefiting from the Wisdom of Others' Experience

Your seasoned performer shares in the human experience of working, feeling, playing and growing in this field — like a mirror that might help predict your future. And this brings me back to something I mentioned early on, when we were talking about differences from generation to generation.

It's true that the events of our youth shape our values and desires. Simply look at my own mother's generation — children of the Great Depression. She never makes a meal without reminding us how much more it would have cost if we had eaten in a restaurant! We relive the ever-present thrift consciousness of her era at every meal. And more recently, we see the impact of the events on September 11th. We now pay greater attention to security and hold a raised apprehension about the possibility of daily blasts to our safety. This awareness affects our risk taking behaviors and sense of adventure.

Despite such differences, though, each generation has aspirations for a fruitful future. In that way, you are just like your parents and their parents before them. You have more in common than you think. Don't believe the trite declarations that the generation before you only wanted a steady paycheck. Just because my own parents worked the same job all their lives, doesn't mean they didn't have dreams. What they accomplished out of the despair of the Great Depression and the ravage of World War II is immense — they passed on to us social safety nets and economic stability that didn't exist before.

As you tap into the dreams of your parents and the seasoned performers you will meet, they will be inspiring, I promise you. This inspiration will contribute to the impact you and your own generation will make.

On balance, if there is an opportunity to talk to seasoned performers and try something out, versus sit and flip through Internet postings — always, always pick the opportunity to connect and to act. This goes back to *Guided Drift*. The more you guide yourself into meeting and talking to people, the more likely you'll find someone who "just happens to know about . . ." and it'll feel like drift and purpose at the same time.

As you begin information interviewing and networking, I want you to concentrate initially on using the questions for seasoned performers. You've done this once early on with a family friend, but refining your questioning skills and getting into someone else's experience is the point of this effort.

The sole purpose of your conversation is to listen to their stories and try to put yourself in their shoes. Try to live in their world for a few minutes. Again, it may be tempting to dismiss some of what they say because they might come from a different generation, or a different background. But they have a truth to tell you about what their world is like. The most ingenious part of your master plan is to talk with seasoned performers, with no agenda other than to experience their experiences — let them be your surrogates.

Create a seasoned performer list and use the prep and questions below for your conversation. I have repeated the instructions for conducting a seasoned performer interview (from Activity 5, page 31). Now that you have become clearer on your *WHAT-WHERE-WHO* you will find that you listen differently to the conversation. And that is how they become groundbreaking conversations.

Activity 32

Seasoned Performer Interview

Conduct a seasoned performer interview. Create an experience where you allow the seasoned performer to serve as your surrogate for the work world you desire to enter. Here's a suggestion for how to call and e-mail your seasoned performer to prepare for the interview.

STEPS

1. **Call** — *"Hi, Joe referred me to you as someone who could help me understand your line of work. I'm interested in looking for opportunities in sustainability, and would love to hear about your career path and the work you do. It will only take twenty minutes. I am particularly interested in hearing about what your work day is like and what your role is in your organization."*

2. **E-mail** — *"Bob, Thank you for agreeing to meet me (on Wednesday, October 10 at 2 p.m. at the Galaxy Coffee House). I'll be wearing a striped shirt, so I should be easy to spot. Thank you so much for your time, I think it will be a fun conversation for both of us."*

3. **Stick to four simple questions** for the interview: (copy the guide sheet on page 34)

   1. What brought you to this career?
   2. What is it like on a day-to-day basis?
   3. What keeps you doing what you're doing?
   4. If you could do something else for a living, what would it be?

4. **Remember to just listen** — no note taking. This is pure conversation. You'll write notes after your seasoned performer leaves.

5. **Ask:** Any ideas of who else I could talk to? Would you be kind enough to refer me? Take notes here!

6. **Pull out your notebook** once your seasoned performer leaves and write your notes.

7. **Follow up** with a hand-written thank you note.

8. **If your interview didn't go the way you thought it should** or could, see the *Resource Center* on *Handling Disappointment* in the *Frustration 101* section for more help.

Even More Contacts

Isn't it nice to know that you're not starting with a blank slate? Let's look at what you already have: starting ideas of names on your *Coffee House Blueprint,* and ideas from your mentor and your seasoned performers. Add to that the referrals you may have from talking to family, co-workers, and friends—and you could have up to a dozen ideas of who to start with right now. If you're not quite there yet, don't worry—I'll get you there.

Building contacts is something like starting a conga line at a wedding reception. You know, that dance where someone invites another person to grab onto their hips, they start tapping their toes in unison, and before you know it, people are linking in and having a great time.

What I like about this image is that people join in and drop out, but somehow it keeps going until it's reached its destination. It works, though, because often someone you know coaxes you into the line—and it's the connection that draws you in. Reaching out and networking work the same way—the closer the connection, the easier it is to link to someone. Once you're connected, it becomes easier and easier to stay connected. You have way more links than you imagine. That notion that everyone is within six degrees of separation from you is pretty accurate.

The other side of reaching out is that you have to work at it. In fact, I recommend you set your sights on working through the list you have, and letting the right people come to you. It's another version of *Guided Drift*. When your message gets out there, it's amazing how the right people start showing up on your path. But you have to work at it — this is where discipline and effort pay off.

If you don't have six or more people on your list you can contact right now, let's change that. You'll get what you want by breaking out of your shyness, lack of confidence, or belief that you don't know how to do this well enough. In fact, this might be a good time to go back and redo Activity 31, page 114 — *Warm up Steps for Information Interviews* — where you take it small step by small step to find someone you can talk to. In addition, review the checklist in Activity 33, below, and find one name to put behind every contact you currently have.

Just so you know that this stuff really works, let me share with you a couple of experiences, that of Sean, and another of my shy friend Matt. Sean is the one who took off for Denver as his WHERE adventure. Once he was there, he connected with a couple of my professional colleagues who lived in the area. Even though neither of them worked in the fields Sean was interested in, I knew they were well acquainted with the region, and guessed they might themselves have friends or acquaintances in his areas of interest. Well, wonder of wonders, both did. As a result of calling and paying each a visit, he got referrals to an oil company and to someone who works for the EPA in Denver — both connected to one of his search areas, environmental sustainability.

Matt, as you recall, is an avid reader and researcher. He wanted to get involved with public radio as a news team researcher. When he approached the local station he found out that an old colleague of his mom's worked where he wanted to intern — and she helped smooth the way for him to make further contacts inside. This resulted in him getting an opportunity to volunteer at the NPR station. It's like turning over a rock, only to find a whole colony of critters living there — a universe you didn't even know existed. That's how the connecting and networking game works. So go see who you can turn up in the next exercise.

Activity 33

Expanding Your Contact List

GO

If your project needs some more resources, write down one name and contact information for each of the following people in your network. You may need to write this out on a separate sheet of paper, because you may have more than one of each kind of person among your contacts.

STEPS

1. **Find one contact** from each of these people who knows something about your WHAT-WHERE-WHO areas of interest and list their contact information on your Contact List.

Mother	*Father*	*Siblings*
Parent's friends	*Parent's co-workers*	*Aunt/uncle*
Grandparents	*Other family*	*Friends*
Mentors	*Classmates*	*School organizations*
Your co-workers	*Neighbors*	*Other associates**
Casual meeting*	*Anyone I forgot*	

   *People you work out with, do hobbies with, hang out with, or even someone you strike up a conversation with in a trusted environment.

2. **Extend the search as far as you can** — include your friends' parents, an old friend you haven't seen in five years.

3. **Once you get the contact names, rank order them** from highest to lowest, based on your best guess about how helpful they might be. Then enter them in your Contact List with all the appropriate information, and begin contacting them in your priority order. Contact even your lower ranked entries — there are always surprises in the least likely places.

A Word about
Information Interview Etiquette

As you get more and more information interviews, remember to be mindful of the basic etiquette of handling the arrangements and the follow-up. Here they are:

Tips on Information Interview Etiquette

1. Make the first contact by phone or in person.

2. Ask for twenty minutes and inform your contact you want to understand more about the line of work she is in.

3. Once the contact has agreed to meet, ask her to identify a convenient time and location (whenever possible try to meet in the contact's workplace — it will give you even more information about working in that type of environment).

4. Be sure you have a correct e-mail address for your contact and physical address for the meeting.

5. Follow up immediately with a confirmation e-mail, and say that you will send a reminder note the day before your planned meeting.

6. Arrive at the meeting place early — try to relax a little, or at least get comfortable in the environment. Remember this person was once exactly where you are — you're creating an opportunity to reminisce about that!

7. However it goes is the way it's supposed to go. Too polished, and you could have a stiff conversation. Too loose, and you won't be taken seriously. Learn as you go to find the right rhythm and approach that works for you.

8. Always ask the contact to do the talking—about interests, experience, and people—following the information interview (page 34) format.

9. Always remember to ask for referrals to other people who might be able to help you.

10. If the contact asks you to talk about your interests, skills, and experience be prepared to draw on the thinking and preparation you have already done. Let her know about your WHAT-WHERE-WHO, about things you have long been passionate about, and what your hopes and aspirations are for the future.

11. Thank the contact for her time that day, and send a hand-written thank you note within twenty-four hours.

Now you have the approach and a list, and you're working it. You even may have already had one or several information interviews. You will run into some bumps as you go, so consult the *Resource Center* on *Frustration 101* to help ease you through.

As you continue to line up information interviews you will begin to notice that some of them feel a little like a job interview. That's common—sometimes an informal conversation can turn into a somewhat more serious discussion of skills and experience. What's great about this is that you are more relaxed in these situations and therefore better able to show off who you are and what you have to offer with little pretense. It's the best way to land an opportunity! A great personal conversation beats a formal discussion any day.

Looking back at Sean and Matt's stories, in both cases the contact that helped seal the deal for each of them was through a close connection. Matt ended up connecting to an old colleague of his mom's, who created a bridge to an internship he wanted. Sean, who was interested in a job in the environment, also had on his original *Coffee House Blueprint* an interest in sports and the outdoors. He happened to see an ad for a marketing assistant with a professional lacrosse league, and when he asked his friend if he or his boss knew anyone in the organization, the boss asked why he wasn't working for him!

As it turned out, Sean's good friend worked for an athletic equipment company, and his boss had just opened a new job. The connections come in funny ways — but proof once again, that asking questions and keeping your ear to the ground opens doors. And *Guided Drift* is always at work.

Managing Your Contact List. Whether you have one information interview going right now or a handful, you will start to notice very quickly that lots of tidbits of information are flying. Whatever system you like to manage them, please, just manage them. I highly recommend you keep everything in one notebook or spreadsheet and update it as soon as you have booked, completed, or followed up on it. You may want to transfer notes you took in the interview to your Contact List so everything is in one place.

This Contact List is your lifeline. It contains the tracks that will take you to your opportunity. Guard it like you would a classic "little black book" — it has information that is precious to your future.

One final note about your list. This is not the time to create a new system or to try to make a major behavior change in how you manage your life. Use what works for you, and remain diligent about consistency and timeliness. Ask someone to help you if you need to — if you're a little scatter-brained, like I can be at times (I get lots of help, between technology and gentle reminders from family and friends).

Staying the Course. Even the best of networks has lulls and some downtime. People don't follow up or respond on your timeline. You think they aren't interested in you because you don't hear from them for a while. These intermissions are natural.

This is your time to breathe and get yourself re-energized. People are busy — even the seasoned performers and mentors who want to help. It's important, though, to persist, without being a pest. Leave five to ten days between your requests, especially the initial ones. Remember, people could be out of the office or on vacation for a week, or buried knee deep in a conference. This gives them the breathing space of a workweek between your requests.

But given all this, there will still be pauses. This is the time to kick up your Pet Project — the one you put in your Project Plan. You really need to see some concrete progress now. And don't beat yourself up for taking a break from your Project Plan. A day or two away from it could help revitalize your perspective.

In addition, this is a good time to tap into the *Resource Center* section on *Movement*. Your brain works best when it is sparked by the energy that your body can deliver. The most important thing right now is to keep moving. As Joseph Campbell says:

> As you proceed through life,
> Following your own path,
> Birds will shit on you.
> Don't bother to brush it off . . .
> Having a sense of humor saves you.

So keep going, don't bother brushing anything off — instead work it out through movement, or your Pet Project, then jump back in when you see an opening in the road.

Finding New Sources of Contacts. Sometimes the cupboard becomes empty and you need to replenish your resources. First, go back to everybody you know and ask for more ideas. Second, look through old address books, Christmas card lists, yearbooks and the like. Third, identify professional or non-profit groups that might have meetings in your area. For example, I just googled "Denver environmental organizations" and found dozens of listings ranging from the Sierra Club to the regional water quality and control board. Now you can start doing things like attending Sierra Club meetings to see who knows who in Denver, or finding out if local municipalities have job listings. This opens up a whole new vista on connections and job opportunities.

This is also a time to keep in close contact with your friends and family. They are the most highly invested in supporting your success, and continued conversations always open up more ideas on what to do next and who you can connect with. The other reason, of course, is that they provide you a shoulder to lean on and a nudge to push you further. Last, but not least, go back to your mentor and a favorite seasoned performer interview. Wherever you feel you made a connection, that is a good field for you to till.

There is one more reason your cupboard could be coming up bare. Is it possible you have the wrong WHAT-WHERE-WHO? That would make it difficult for you to make a meaningful connection with your contacts. If you suspect this may be the case, check out the *Resource Center* on *WHAT-WHERE-WHO Now*? There, I'll help you decipher if you're just going through a mini crisis of confidence, or if you want to seriously reconsider your WHAT-WHERE-WHO. If you've thought about this, and decided that you're on the right track, but just stuck in some mud, then you may want to move things along by trying out some new things.

Trying out New Things

As I've mentioned before, I have a strong bias for action that exposes you to meeting and working with new people and different kinds of careers. Even if you know your WHAT arena, this kind of exposure will give you experience that can lead to new insights about your WHAT. It doesn't hurt, either, that it feeds your connections, replenishes your resource pool for information interviews, and helps you know more about yourself.

What does this look like? And why would you take on additional activities that might keep you from doing more information interviews that could lead you to a job interview? Three reasons:

1) You need some experience, even if it's in a related field
2) You need a stronger source of contacts in your field
3) You need to make some money while you continue looking

Below, I describe several different kinds of activities that serve as try-outs and how they might show up in your life.

Try-outs

1. More seasoned performer interviews. Believe it or not, at the lowest level of activity on this scale of try-out activities are the old seasoned performer interviews. This is because you are experiencing them as a "surrogate" for the actual work. Continue to find more of these, as this exposure will continue to widen your knowledge of different kinds of opportunities in your field of interest.

2. Shadowing. Shadowing is probably the oddest sounding among these actions I recommend because people do it the most infrequently, but shadowing is a great opportunity. I think most people don't have the guts to ask for it. So get up the guts, and if you find somebody doing something that you would really like to understand better, ask if you can spend a day with her at work.

Sean had a great shadowing experience early in his searching days in Denver. He attended a regional one-day conference on environmental sustainability and met some people that install solar panels. He arranged an invitation to come see what that work was all about. He ended up spending the better part of a day on the roof watching an installation and talking about the world of solar energy. It was a great day, especially because he found out that wasn't for him! The best part is that he witnessed the work in action, and had a first hand understanding of it.

So that's all it is. It's like take your kid to work day, now that you're all grown up. You're asking a trusted contact, who does something you're interested in, to take you to work that day. You get a sense of what that world is like. Yes, it's one day out of many, but not only do you get a taste of what your shadow mentor goes through, but you get to interact with people doing other kinds of jobs. You're touching it — like a sports try-out. You're also experiencing the WHERE — the environment. Do you like the tone, the pace, the sound of this place? You're in the performance, but like a dress rehearsal, it's a precursor for you to the actual work.

Arranging a shadow experience is a little different from most other activities. You'll find at the end of this list of try-out recommendations an activity that assists you in setting up a shadowing experience.

3. Volunteering and interning. Whether you're still in college or not, if you have a clear WHAT interest — intern in it, paid or unpaid. Internships can be had after college, even if they're not official. And volunteering in an area of interest will get you just as far. Even if you need to earn money, don't shy away from volunteering. Beth, a friend of mine, spent a summer during college stocking in a local department store at night while she worked several days a week for the Sierra Club. She got some great experience in community activism, policymaking and environmental protection, and managed to earn money at the same time.

Volunteering in community organizations gives you experience working on community teams, where you can get connected to people who are interested in the same things as you. You work side by side with them and begin to hear their stories and learn from them. This is an unbeatable connection to your WHAT-WHERE-WHO. In addition, you gain real experience, and a place on the inside track of who knows who in this world. This helps you stock up on resources for connecting and networking. For Beth, it led to an internship the following summer as a soil sample collector. This was just the motive force that drove her towards graduate work in geology and a career in environmental protection.

4. Part-time jobs. Occasionally there are part-time jobs available directly in your interest area, and often you can create them. Matt managed to combine his volunteer work at NPR with a part-time job assisting in legal research for a law firm. This is a one-two power punch — the flexibility and earning of a part-time job, combined with exposure in the volunteer job.

129

Once you've shown your capabilities, people will be open to creating jobs that connect an organizational need with your talents. That's why working in volunteer jobs is so great—people get to see how you work and what your skills and talents are. Doors then swing open so much easier when there is familiarity with you and confidence that you can do what you say.

If you start out as an intern for the Sierra Club doing database work, before you know it you could land some paid hours for them. Maybe you don't want to build databases all your life, but this kind of part-time job boosts your resume and credibility, and most importantly helps you make even deeper connections in the environmental protection world. And if you're an environmental science major like Beth, this is a golden connection.

5. Temp jobs. As you look for your calling and next opportunity, sometimes you run into uncertainty and confusion. The more you talk to people, or even the less motivated you are to talk to people because of your uncertainty, the more you realize you're not ready or you're unsure about your WHAT. At this point you have two options (assuming you need to make a living): 1) take a temporary job; 2) or take any job that somewhat fits or looks interesting.

Let's talk temp jobs first. Temp jobs are great! I've done it in my career, so I speak first hand of what it can get you. When I did it, I went in with no expectations other than to make some money before my wedding, and ended up with a contact that got me my first teaching job. Surprising things happen when you're loose and relaxed! There's that *Guided Drift* thing again.

But I have also seen temp jobs do many other things for people. First, if you're unsure, a temp job gets you out there working—no matter what it is. You're meeting new people, learning a skill, and finding out what a particular business is like. If you're highly unsure of what you want, temping is a great avenue. You can switch up jobs every two or three months. I do recommend you try to stay long enough in a temp situation to get to know what you like about it and what you don't like about it.

Temping also gets you out of the house. Sometimes I recommend that people temp during their search to put some urgency and momentum back into the process. Even, in fact especially, if the job ends up being something you don't like — you've learned a lot, and have even more motivation to focus on what does make you happy. Basically, temping is on-the-job training — about the work, about you and about what calls to you. Don't be afraid to go for it.

6. Try out a job. You might need to take action if you're unsure about what you want, or realize it's time to get out and make some money. You can take the job that gets offered, even if it's not exactly in your sweet spot, or dead center on your self-described WHAT.

Look, there are no absolutes in life. In fact, *Guided Drift* is in play all the time. Holding out for the perfect job is simply holding out on you. Experience, mixing it up — these are the things that will take you closer to your desired WHAT.

There is no way to predict what your magic elixir of steps will be to help you express all your talents, passion, and skills. The experience of a seasoned performer shows you how someone else did it, but your path won't be exactly the same. Nor should it be — if it were, then it wouldn't be your unique path, would it? Good or bad, each experience tells you something about what you like, what you're good at, what kinds of people you want to be around, and what settings work best for you.

Denver Sean took a career side trip before he initiated his adventure out West. Working in D.C., he decided to try out the legal world, since one of the WHAT areas he had been considering for a while was to become a lawyer. He ended up at a very prestigious firm that specializes in class action suits. Working as a paralegal, he interacted on a daily basis with partners and senior associates at the firm. The work, though, was detailed and isolating. Even though he was good at managing the details, he needed interaction and the opportunity to be part of a team.

A year on the job confirmed that this was not the life for him. But the year also afforded him time to learn the documentation and follow-up skills to manage large cases. In addition, he now had some very specialized skills to fall back on in a pinch. Today, he applies those skills every day as he supports the sales and quality efforts of a sports equipment company. And the best part is, he is an integral part of a team, getting to work outside occasionally, supporting lacrosse events, and learning a ton about running a small company.

Listen to that anchor inside you. Action will help you move to the next step. You can't run a marathon if you can't run a 5K. So take the small steps — especially if you find yourself in a stuck place and need to get pulled out of the mud. If you're stuck pretty deep, we'll be talking more about managing yourself in the next chapter. Even more help can be found in the *Resource Center* on *Unsticking Stuckness.*

In summary, don't be afraid of tests and try-outs. The more you get experience, the more you'll know about yourself and your best fit, and the better you'll perform in the next interview. You become more valuable to prospective employers as you gain a variety of experiences, and you'll find the process to be more fun and fulfilling. And each of these experiences prepares you for the job interview. Leonard Mlodinow, in *The Drunkard's Walk: How Randomness Rules Our Lives*, puts it this way:

> "What I've learned, above all, is to keep marching forward because the best news is that since chance does play a role, one important factor in success is under our control: the number of at bats, the number of chances taken, the number of opportunities seized. For even a coin weighted toward failure will sometimes land on success. Or as the IBM pioneer Thomas Watson said, 'If you want to succeed, double your failure rate.'"

Below is the activity that will help you set up a shadowing experience. This one is a little different from volunteering or getting a part-time job. But you can certainly use some of the techniques of this set-up process for getting yourself more chances through a volunteer or intern position.

Activity 34

Arranging to Shadow

GO

Set up an opportunity to spend a day with someone in a job that interests you, so you can understand it better and make stronger connections with people in that line of work.

STEPS

1. **Set up the Shadow Experience**

   Make a phone call: *"Hi Joe, I met you at the conference and I'm really interested in what it takes to be in the green building business. I know you have some people on your staff who do the job I think I'm interested in. I was wondering if I could come and shadow them for a day? I'll just sit in the background and observe, trying to understand if this is the kind of work I would like."*

   Follow up with an e-mail confirmation.

2. **Manage the Shadow Day**

   a) Talk to as many different people as you can (while respecting people's need to get their work done)

   b) As you meet different people and you get the chance, ask: Why did you come to this job? What makes you stay?

   c) Take notes when you can on what you are noticing about the environment (steady, stressed, open to ideas, rigid, how people talk to each other, etc.)

3. **Make notes about your day** right after you leave — what you liked, didn't like, etc.

4. **Don't forget to ask for information interview referrals** from your host, and remember to write a thank you note to the person you shadowed and the person who helped you arrange the shadowing (if different).

On the Road to an Interview

As you head down the road, getting closer to interviews for job opportunities, you will encounter your internal and external obstacles. We'll talk about internal obstacles in the next chapter, *Managing Yourself*. External obstacles include the influence of others (from parents to social pressures at large) and the very real need to earn money. I would never suggest that you give away your passion, or let your heart be stolen for the opportunity to merely make money. That said, I am also a practical person.

If the obstacle is earning money, then go ahead and wait tables, do construction, take a temp job — open yourself to any kind of job that has flexibility in it. These are the ways you can hold on to your passion, but still take care of yourself. Moving these kinds of obstacles can also create opportunities. If you're out there earning money while you're still pursuing your passion, *Guided Drift* has occasion to sweep in your direction.

The Interview. Now that you're in the middle of action, there are a couple of things you should start noticing. You're getting closer to talking to people about job possibilities that intersect with your purpose. If you're not headed that way, then something is missing, you're hiding from yourself, or you're not really into this. It's time to circle back to do some more reflection, or jump ahead and look into managing yourself in the next chapter.

If, on the other hand, things are starting to rev up, then start putting yourself in the position of moving your information interviews to the next level. With your experience, you can begin to be more pointed in inquiring about specific openings, and getting referred to people in companies that are hiring. Also remember that jobs at the beginning of a career ladder can often be found in small companies that aren't doing massive recruitment outreach. That's why the network is so important. These are opportunities that are found by word of mouth — in your case, the mouths of the people you are connecting with.

All that said, the *Resource Center* on *Job Search Stuff* will point you to a set of focused, time-proven pointers on interviewing and resume writing.

As long as you have a decent resume, with all the background work you've done, your resume will land in the right hands. Simply think about the interview as a conversation with someone who needs something from you—and an opportunity for you to make a choice. If you find yourself getting close to choosing, and want more advice on that right now, you can jump to Chapter 8: *Choosing*.

Bring It In. At some point you will have one or more opportunity offers in front of you. Now you have another choice. While this may feel like the biggest choice you've ever made, remember—this is the next step on your path, and you have many more choices ahead of you. This next job is another question set, which you will answer. The idea here is to take in everything you know about the choices you are making. Pay attention and know what is important to you—your WHO-WHERE environment, and your WHAT that draws on your skills, passion and enthusiasm. Follow your intuition about yourself and your needs over your anxiety and excitement.

PAY ATTENTION

Needs and wants

What's your next move?

Heads Up. We'll dive more deeply into this in Chapter 8 on *Choosing*. You're ready to transition to the *Docking* phase. As you dock you will be preparing for what's to come. So we'll start by focusing on managing yourself as you shift into a new mode. In the next chapter we'll talk about different ways people respond to stress, and help you tap into the coping mechanisms you have, as well as build some new ones.

Phase III: DOCKING

Engaging the World

Managing Yourself

You've been working hard, contacting people, following up, and reviewing what's working and what's not working for you. This takes some serious energy, and you can feel good about contacts you have made — whether few or many. Energy sweeps over you at times, and at others it drains away, as if someone pulled the plug on you. This is all very normal. Don't forget, you're taking an active hand in creating the building blocks of your future — this is Olympic level training!

It's now time to think about how you can best manage yourself as you progress towards docking in a new place and role. This is a pause, where you can reflect on how to manage the stresses and worries of this transition. Consider:

> "The way that we see things today does not have to be the way we saw them yesterday. That is because the situations, our relationships to them, and we ourselves have changed in the interim. This notion of constant change suggests that we do not have to be discouraged."
>
> —T. K. V. Desikachar

PAY ATTENTION

Pause-abilities

What's your next move?

My friend and mentor, Pamela Curlee, calls times like this "pause-abilities." Slowing down, reflecting, and paying attention to our bodies, our minds, and our emotions frees up the space to explore what else is possible.

This is the place to take a time-out. We'll explore ways to help you get unstuck when things are dragging, then we'll end the chapter with a discussion of what to do if you've got the wrong WHAT-WHERE-WHO. Even that can be a good thing, so don't panic — it's another port of call on the *Guided Drift* journey. The activities in this chapter help keep you invested in the game, especially in the slow times. Use the ones you need, leave the rest behind.

Redirecting Your Self-talk

You've chosen a focus and the fog is beginning to clear. You have talked to your seasoned performers, done a little research, and now you wake up with night sweats wondering if you're on the right track. You may even find yourself bobbing and weaving, considering all kinds of options. What's going on?

First, let's define bob and weave. Like a boxer avoiding the face-off, you duck from your focus. This is where you think you've figured out your WHAT-WHERE-WHO, but then find yourself jabbing at every chance that floats by. You start following leads like a dog in a city park — running, running everywhere. If you're chasing every lead that comes your way, despite the homework you did on *you,* then you're bobbing and weaving. Either 1) you have the wrong WHAT (or WHERE or WHO); or 2) you're not ready to commit, and need to try some things out first; or 3) you have a bad case of the 3Fs: you're in Flight, Fight or Freeze mode — letting the stress and worries overcome you.

So talk to yourself. Do you really not yet know what you want? Are you running away from commitment to a pretty good fit? Or are you feeling frenzied, confused, and overwhelmed?

With these questions in mind, let's look at the process of self-talk a little more closely. As I've mentioned before, the conversations we have in our heads on a daily basis determine how we live our lives. Gandhi once said,

Your beliefs become your thoughts,
your thoughts become your words,
your words become your actions,
your actions become your habits,
your habits become your values,
and your values become your destiny.

In Activity 35, you will take some time to reflect on how your beliefs turn into self-talk. It's a chance to look at your "pause-abilities." We all have continuous loop conversations in our heads that affect how we behave, and how we respond to what's going on in our environment. This activity will help you examine the kinds of conversations going on in your head more closely.

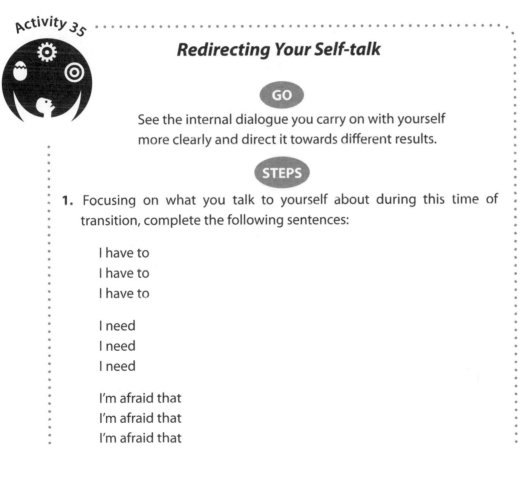

Activity 35

Redirecting Your Self-talk

GO

See the internal dialogue you carry on with yourself
more clearly and direct it towards different results.

STEPS

1. Focusing on what you talk to yourself about during this time of transition, complete the following sentences:

   I have to

   I have to

   I have to

   I need

   I need

   I need

   I'm afraid that

   I'm afraid that

   I'm afraid that

2. Now go back to these sentences and change the words in each of the groupings as follows (actually cross them out and rewrite them):

> *I have to:* Change to *I want to*
> *I need:* Change to *I choose*
> *I'm afraid that:* Change to *I doubt that*

3. What changed for you with this wording change?

4. How does this different mode of self-talk affect the dialogue you have with yourself?

5. What are the greatest stressors and/or fears that popped out for you as you changed these statements?

6. The words *I want*, *I choose*, and *I doubt* all move you from the victim mentality of external requirements, needs and fears to the internal ownership of aspiration, choice and doubt (here doubt is movement on the continuum from fear to hope). Given that:

> What one statement, changed to the words of responsibility, choice and acceptance (I want, I choose, I doubt) is most key for you to imbed in your self-talk every day? (See the conversation that follows for my personal example of how this process has affected my own work.)

Here is how examining my self-talk affected the major change I undertook in my career. When I began this project, I sought help from my coach Pamela, and used a combination of physical movement and goal setting — a process called Brain Gym®. She helped me understand how my fear of being 5 percent short in energy and enthusiasm for my project was in my control.

My statement was: I'm afraid that I have 95 percent of what it takes to bring this project to life, but that my 5 percent fear factor will overtake my confidence. As I worked with Pamela, looking at my self-talk on this matter, I eventually changed my statement to: I doubt my 95 percent confidence will be overtaken by my 5 percent fear.

This revolutionized my approach to my work. I began to recognize on a daily basis how I would use excuses of other responsibilities in my life to run away from biting the bullet, facing my "5 percent fear factor" and dedicating the time to work on this project. I learned how much "Flight" was my escape from stress and fear.

Stress Response — How to Deal

Let's look more closely at the stress responses Flight, Fight and Freeze — the 3Fs. They come from a deep part of our brains that works to keep us safe. We share these instincts with all our cousins in the animal kingdom.

Some animals fight first — like a tiger; some freeze first — remember the saying "play possum"?; and some animals flee when threatened — think of the gazelle. It's important to remember that like our animal friends, we have all three responses in our repertoire, but we usually do one better than the others. Deer, for example, will freeze first when threatened, but then they can run awfully fast, and will fight if they have to.

The irony of these stress responses today is that instead of fighting off a threatening wooly mammoth, we use them when a report is late, our boss is upset with us, or we're following a slow-poke in traffic when we're late for a meeting. Your heart pounds, you perspire, your breathing gets shallow and your muscles tighten. When you really need to run from that mammoth or prepare to fight it, this is great stuff. Senses sharpen, time slips into slow motion, and you become impervious to pain. But when you're sitting at your desk, you are literally stewing in your own juices — stirring up hormones and chemicals that will more likely harm than help.

Putting the 3Fs in Their Place. In your plan you face outside and inside roadblocks. While you can't ignore outside obstacles, it's the inside roadblocks we have to watch for during major transitions. They range from resentment, to anger, to avoidance, to running away — and many things in between. Our need for security often leads us to create overprotective ways of handling scary situations.

We flee, we fight, or we freeze. You are showing up with one or more of these reactions right now. If you're not feeling your heart racing, your palms sweaty, churning feelings of lows and highs, then you're probably not stepping out to the edge of your potential. If you are feeling these things — then good for you, you're definitely in the zone for change. So let's figure out how to cope with these reactions and put them to good use.

First, accept. That's why I've been asking you to pay attention. You're perfectly human. Next, notice. Notice when your heart is skipping, when you're biting your nails, playing with your hair (my fallback), when a foot or fingers are tapping, when you're angry, when you feel like a pent up tiger, when you're tired for no reason, eating too much (or too little), or overly aggressive. These can be signs of stress. Let's look at the three ways of handling fear to help you figure out where you have a tendency to get stuck.

PAY ATTENTION

Habits

What's your next move?

What Is Flight? You may be in flight if you run away from conflict, watch too much TV, or even work out too much. Running away can take some very "responsible"-looking twists — like my mother needs help, or I need to donate some time to this fundraiser. It's all very noble sounding, but the reality is, you are making a choice to spend your time somewhere other than your named priority.

The importance of conscious choice-making shows up, and you choose something else over working on this life-changing opportunity you are trying to create. Know that you are making a statement to self and others that it is more important to take care of other things than change your life. Now, you will say, "Oh, but life happens, and there are things I have to do." Of course things happen — why do you think I said you don't want to work on this ten hours a day? Because life happens. Just notice what you are fleeing towards.

How Do You Deal with Flight? While I've had enough years under my belt to get pretty good at all 3Fs, I am a particularly adept fleer. Here are the things that help me, and I've seen help others. First, create a priority list of the key things that are important to you. Ask those closest to you to help you stay focused.

Next, ask yourself, "What am I doing *now* that contributes to my project?" Try to do that every workday. But don't micro-manage your schedule, or you probably won't have the energy to keep it up. Use calendars and reminders for *weekly* priorities. If you use electronic tools to help, be careful your entries don't become wallpaper, which you end up ignoring.

You want to be very conscious and deliberate in how you think about putting time to good use. Sticky notes with reminders on your fridge or computer help too. So does asking someone to remind you.

I can tell you, from my experience as a designer and writer, that it is easy to tell others that you're not busy when you don't have external deadlines imposed. I am incredibly busy when I'm writing and designing. What's different is that my schedule is flexible. It's actually exactly what is happening to you right now if you don't have another job besides changing your life and finding a new career opportunity.

Your time is spoken for — don't give it away. Fleers must guard their time like misers. We often find it difficult to say no to others, and then become resentful when a day has gone by — busy, but unproductive on our goals.

The last thing for fleers, is to pace ourselves. Other projects and people need our attention — give it to them in adequate doses. Then look for the warning signs of flight: too many days pass without progress, we start making excuses for how busy we are with interferences in our life, or we start feeling sluggish because we've been running too hard in the wrong direction. This is the time to gently ask, "What can I do *now* to move my project ahead?" No need to beat yourself up.

In summary, if flight is your game, here are your key tips:

Tips for Coping with Flight

1. Don't assume your schedule is infinitely flexible.
2. Pay attention to escape time. Ask why? How much is enough?
3. Come up with a standard line when someone asks you to donate your time to a new cause. For example, "This is very interesting, but I need to think about it and consult with my family (boyfriend, girlfriend, work schedule, etc.)."

What Is Fighting? Fight, when we're talking about life stressors, usually shows up as frenzy. You "attack" your problems, you "have" to get all these things done, there's "never" enough time. For example, you're so overwhelmed by the task of creating a great resume, that you can't find time to have a seasoned performer conversation, much less find a mentor. Your schedule is booked, you're overloaded, and you can only do the minimum.

Any form of resistance equals fighting. The self-talk starts sounding like this: "This isn't good enough; I can't start over; this doesn't fit; there's too much to do; these activities are a waste of time; I'll never get a job by just talking to people. . . ." If you experience a lot of this, you are a fighter.

My friend Pamela demonstrated this fighting/frenzied approach to change in a workshop. It's the old Three Stooges routine — where you nail one foot down and pedal around it in circles with your other foot. Around and around you go; you're busy, but you're not getting anywhere. Flipping through the Internet is a good example, as is rewriting your resume or cover letter a dozen times, or not venturing out of a small network. Busy pedaling, but no progress.

How Do You Deal with Fighting Mode? You find a calm, cool, objective coach who will be your rock and your guide. You also face yourself. You journal a lot and you move a lot to get rid of the excess energy. This is especially helpful to fighters who need outlets for their energy.

The key for fighters is to find one or more objective anchors, people who can help them see their frenzied state. The frenzy sometimes just looks busy — but busy with things that aren't *so* important. Keeping a priority list front and center helps you focus on the important stuff. And remember, we have all three coping methods in our DNA — fighting can slip into freezing or fleeing very easily.

Tips for Coping with Fight Mode

1. Put some "time-out" breaks on your schedule — yes, actually write them in. It may sound ridiculous to you, but try it.

2. Keep track of how many times in a given day you use your "attack line." By this I mean, language like "I can squeeze that in"; "I *have* to do this"; "*I'll* take care of it."

3. Write "Three Stooges" somewhere that you will see it — and once a day, ask yourself: When did I do this today? How often did I do this today? Why did I do this today?

And when you notice this behavior go right back to Tip 1 — take a time-out so you can see what you are doing. Then calm down, get focused, and instead of attacking your problem, use the ASK-CHOOSE-ACT approach (see page 58 to revisit the steps).

What Is Freezing? Sometimes freeze doesn't look a lot different from flight because it's another form of avoidance. This one, though, is the "deer in headlights" experience. You say you're going to get something done and you just sit and stare. You literally get nothing done. Yes, you may be thinking — but there's no documentation, no evidence, no action. It can show up as pondering and deliberation — thorough thinking and reflection. But it can become analysis paralysis — an overabundance of thinking. Even the deer — who is especially good at freezing — must move, and fast, to save itself.

How Do You Deal with Freezing? You're going to need action even more if you tend to be a freezer. You want to put small tasks in front of you. You want to talk to people who are close to you, who reduce your anxiety and encourage you little step by little step to move forward. The signs of freezing include attempting to get something done, and getting no results, stalling for days on a task that takes minutes, missing deadlines, worrying and fretting endlessly.

This can also look like procrastination—which is a moderate form of freezing. Think about it. When the really simple things don't happen, you know you are in freeze mode. The way out of this is very small tasks that build up confidence—keeping adequately busy—not frenzied, but at a reasonable work pace. It's key not to overload yourself. This is where that old Chinese proverb about a journey of 1,000 miles comes in handy. You do it one step at a time.

Tips for Coping with Freezing

1. Set a weekly meeting with a friend to do a progress check on how you're doing.
2. Set a time limit for how long you let yourself mope around—two hours, two days, two weeks. Just the idea of a time limit helps.
3. Put aside your worry for fifteen minutes and make one phone call, send one e-mail, or take a short walk.

Moving Past Our Security Blankets

Are you a fleer, a fighter, or a freezer? Sometimes we can be all three, but we have a tendency to be one more than the others. In the next activity, you will identify your primary means of reacting to stress, then put a plan together to develop coping mechanisms.

Coping with Stress: Understanding Your 3Fs

Understand your typical responses to stress —
Flight, Fight or Freeze — and identify ways to cope
with this stress.

1. **Complete the survey on page 150** by reading the descriptions and rank ordering your responses from 1 to 3, with 1 being your most usual and customary response, 2, your second response, and 3 the response you use the least.

2. **If you need help getting clear, talk to a trusted friend**, family member, or one of your mentors.

3. **If one behavior describes you especially well, circle it.**

4. **Describe what you do** when you first respond to a stressful situation. For example, as a fleer, you might play too many video games, volunteer your time too much, or get too much exercise.

   How about your second response?

5. **What one coping mechanism will you start using today** (like sticky notes, meditation, calendar, journaling, physical activity, using coaches)? How will that help you?

6. **How will you know you're making progress?**

COPING WITH STRESS

Response	Description	Typical Behaviors	Order
Flight	Run for my life	Do anything else Run away through other activities Remove myself from the line of fire Bury myself in another project	#_____
Fight	Attack	Pounce on projects Get keyed up Do things in overdrive Work to exhaustion	#_____
Freeze	Stop and play dead	Avoid dealing Become invisible Do nothing Brood	#_____

Antidotes to Overload

We each have antidotes to overload, we just have to watch them when they get to the edge of helping or hurting. A little TV is OK, endless hours are not. My antidotes include yoga, walking, running, and sometimes to veg out in front of the TV, especially a favorite movie that has predictability, a rhythm and a soothing sense. I also know that my antidotes can become my outs. If I find myself loafing in front of the TV too many days in a row, a little mild sadness or depression has set in. I may need to either give myself permission to take a break, accept the lull and not beat myself up over it, or dive into some of my antidotes.

I hope you've been using some of them through this process. Keep it up. If you need to remind yourself of them, put them into your plan. I do. This results in a much stronger habit of exercise, balance and stress release for me.

PAY ATTENTION

Time to rewire

What's your next move?

Stuck can be good news when you're paying attention — the frustration it creates can raise your awareness of the need for change, if you're listening. When you pick up and change, you're picking up those neurons in your brain that formed old habits and moving them somewhere else. You need time to reshape yourself, similar to the way strengthening a muscle for a particular motion takes practice and discipline. Getting unstuck boils down to these three things:

Tips for Getting Unstuck

1. Self-talk that provides awareness, insight and hope

2. Time to think — whether it's quiet time, a long run, meditation, or writing in a journal

3. Action — it can be small in the low moments — like writing in your journal, picking up the phone and calling a mentor or taking a nap so you can refresh and rewire your brain. Or it can be big — finishing your Pet Project, nailing an important interview.

Being aware of these and asking someone to help pull you up off the couch if you're a freezer, help you stop battling yourself if you're a fighter, and to focus you if you're a fleer running away — that's the essence of coping skills. *Unsticking Stuckness* in the *Resource Center* can help you even more.

Staying in the Game

You're going to have watershed moments, days when things will go really well. Thank God for those days. In between the watershed days, though, will be the continuous progress days.

As our glacier-climbing guide told us, the best way to hike a mountain is by putting one foot in front of the other, and not continually looking down at your feet. You scan the path ahead, lift up your head, and keep moving forward based on the plan you have and the continual sweep you do of the terrain every five to ten steps. This way you're not plodding through the process, and with your head up you can enjoy the scenery and the experience.

Let's turn to the present moment. How is this a game worth playing for you right now? What will keep this alive and exciting for you? What's going to keep your head up and continue drawing you forward? You have to shed your old skin before you can get a new one — the only thing is, people didn't warn you that it can be itchy, uncomfortable, and downright irritating at times.

You're already moving. You've been talking to your mentors, to the seasoned performers, and you will continue to converse and interview. The plan here is to keep you in the game.

Activity 37

Staying in the Game

GO

Keep yourself motivated by reinforcing why you are doing this discovery and how you can stay on your game.

STEPS

Answer the following questions. Discuss with mentors and friends as needed.

1. Why is this a game worth playing?

2. What will keep you in the game?

3. If it doesn't feel like a game worth playing, what would make it one?

4. What's important *now*?

As you retool and refocus, go back to the concept we've already talked about — asking good questions. How do you keep upping the ante, asking specific questions that will take you to a specific next step? Give yourself something concrete to do next. Remember, this is about momentum. So keep it going by stopping and asking what's important NOW from time to time.

Plan to Be Surprised

As you look at your WHAT-WHERE-WHO and you continue reaching out, interviews will start turning up opportunities for you. Your WHAT, for example, might be the whole world of improving the environment. You'll then be challenged to clarify the particular opportunity inside of the bigger WHAT arena — is it biodiesel fuel, solar panels, local government, green building, organic farming, policy and law? If you're passionate about this, you'll push through and narrow down your choices, remembering to consider the role that WHERE and WHO play. In short, you'll pick a place to start.

It's also possible that the choice will find you, in the form of a job offer. Now you ask yourself, is that a good enough place to start? Remember, it's all about finding some place to start and something to DO that fits you. All I know is that sometimes it's the surprises that take you down the best path. So while you're planning, don't forget to plan to be surprised.

What If I Have the Wrong WHAT-WHERE-WHO? You've looked at stressors and coping skills, and considered other things that might be causing some bobbing and weaving. You may be left, all the same, with an uncertainty about your WHAT or WHERE or WHO. If you believe you need to rethink this, go to the *Resource Center* and explore the *WHAT-WHERE-WHO Now?* section. There you will get recommendations on how to circle back and re-cast your WHAT-WHERE-WHO.

This may not be the kind of surprise you wanted to see, but try to look at it this way: "Well, what a surprise. After doing some soul-searching, I haven't quite got it. Maybe it's time to go DO something, and quit thinking so much."

Bring It In. Get your bearings before you go back into action. By now you're realizing that either 1) you've reinforced your WHAT-WHERE-WHO; 2) you need to get more experience to figure it out; or 3) your WHAT-WHERE-WHO is not on target. Congratulations for paying attention.

If you take a job because you're nervous, and need to do something — go ahead. It's part of your path to entering the right WHAT-WHERE-WHO arena. This is one way to gain experience, just like Sean did by working in a law firm for a year.

Another possibility is that a key part of your WHAT-WHERE-WHO is stability and security. If this is a high need for you, then this steadiness is part of what you have to offer the world. Accept that as part of who you are and go for it. Remember, this is *Guided Drift*. Your WHAT-WHERE-WHO will come to you, because you're paying attention and working it.

This is a circular process. That means you try something, then figure out how it's working. Then you try a little something more, and see what you've learned. You are so far ahead of where you started — just by paying attention, your alertness will carry you far.

And remember, as I've said before, you make the decision, then you make the decision right. The truth is, you have a lifetime to grow and develop, and a decision to take a job or choose a new city "for now" — as long as you're paying attention — can be the perfect amount of drift, with your anchor in place.

PAY ATTENTION

Heart

What's your next move?

Heads Up. You've got a cadre of people willing to help you, and a tool kit full of gadgets to keep you on your path — from stress coping skills, to self-assessment instruments, to a process that will get you to your destination. Your task now is to keep working the process — *Launch-Discovery-Docking* — until you get docked.

For some this may mean revisiting the key choices you have to make about your WHAT-WHERE-WHO. For others, it means creating the breakthrough you might yet need, on understanding your past, present and future possibilities. Even if you circle back now to reassess some of those choices and required breakthroughs — exasperating as this may be — two steps back may be your way forward. So when you're ready, the next chapter takes you into the last part of the *Docking* process. Now it's time to choose the WHAT-WHERE-WHO and leap to the next stage of your life.

Choosing

You've put yourself on a path; you're on a roll right now. You've been talking to people in coffee shops, on the phone, and in the office. Hints of opportunities and maybe even a job offer or two have started coming in. And now it's time to make more choices.

Elements of a Good Choice

Good choices have a lot in common with good questions. Bold leaps are only made on the heels of much practice and many steps of preparation. This is one more step on your path.

The choices that shape your life will feel right in your gut:

1. Good choices will embrace your WHAT-WHERE-WHO nature.

2. Good choices will respond to these three inquiries:
   1) Does it help me follow my calling?
   2) Will this choice move me forward?
   3) Does it meet my needs?

While it's great if you can answer all the parts of 1 and 2 above positively, every opportunity may not be all of these things. Getting two out of three isn't bad. Remember, we're not looking for perfection, we're looking for progress. The reality of most job offers is that they rarely meet all your requirements. They also pop up at the most unexpected moments. The one you thought you nailed doesn't pan out, and the one you thought was so-so, turns into an opportunity. *Guided Drift* continues to work on you. With your solid anchor of clearly defined WHAT-WHERE-WHO, and a thorough knowledge of your past, present, and desired futures, the right opportunities will wander your way.

Take our example of Fred Rogers, a strong believer in the concept of *Guided Drift*. You want to talk about a person who followed his bliss, accepted that there were various futures for him, and left an indelible imprint on television media? He would be that.

Jump to the twenty-first century, and we find Steve Jobs — more evidence of *Guided Drift* at work. Here's a guy who got fired from the company he started, becoming a very public failure. But, as he tells the story, it turned out to be the best thing that ever happened to him. He realized that he still loved what he did, and his exit freed him up to be more creative than ever. Without that jolt, his highly creative period at the technology company NeXT (which he founded) and Pixar (the company that produced the first computer animated movie *Toy Story)* would never have happened. As he describes getting fired:

> "It was awful tasting medicine, but I guess that patient needed it. Sometimes life hits you in the head with a brick. Don't lose faith. I'm convinced that the only thing that kept me going was that I loved what I did. You've got to find what you love. And that is as true for your work as it is for your lovers. Your work is going to fill a large part of your life and the only way to be truly satisfied is to do what you believe is great work. And the only way to do great work is to love what you do. If you haven't found it yet, keep looking.

Don't settle. As with all matters of the heart, you'll know when you find it. And, like any great relationship, it just gets better and better as the years roll on. So keep looking until you find it. Don't settle."

What great examples both Jobs and Rogers provide for us in the twenty-first century, where technology changes so fast it introduces new kinds of jobs every few years. Rogers tested out that new medium of the 1950s called television, and ended up leaving an everlasting mark of excellence in children's television productions. Jobs hung on to what he loved, and kept up the creativity, despite outward signs of failure.

Each man understood his anchor. Between their love of their work, and their deep passion for learning and development, when we unwind their life stories, it's no wonder each became an icon in his field. It shows *Guided Drift* at work, where each trusted his intuition enough to let the drift take him to the right place.

Intention versus Forcing

The crossing points can sometimes hit us when we least expect it. A job opportunity comes up that isn't exactly what we had in our line of sight. It feels like a coincidence or serendipity. It's time to remember the anchor and the bearings you have worked out. It is possible, too, that you feel a need to take this job — whether you feel you need the money, the experience, or to be settled somewhere for a while. Sometimes we need to bump into things in order to learn more about ourselves, our needs, and what drives us.

If you thought I was going to tell you some absolute tried and true rules about which job to take and why, well, such mandates don't exist. All the hype you read and hear about foolproof ways to figure out your life, your calling, and how to find your next job, is artificial. What does exist is the anchor inside of you — and this takes us back to intention versus forcing.

An intention is a leaning, a direction that we create which is very different from pushing something to happen. You have been discovering that sense of intention as you've worked through this process. The opposite experience of feeling forced is common to us all — the gnawing feeling when others have nudged us, pushed us into something we agree to do, but against our better instincts. We comply, though, because we want to please, or at least get some pressure off our backs.

Intention works differently. It's like a river, smooth, steady, and strong enough to forge new courses. What's your intention? If you put out your intention, it's like putting a message in a bottle with the expectation that it will be picked up somewhere, somehow. This is different from getting up one morning with steel armor and a sword, and declaring "I'm going to get a job," by looking on the Internet, and writing cover letters. Push, push, fight, shove. This kind of pushing goes against the grain of your intention.

I'm talking here about forcing yourself to do something that doesn't feel right, that doesn't match your anchor or your declared WHAT-WHERE-WHO. Can you get a job that way? Sure you can. What will the result be? I don't know. It's entirely possible you could push and force your way into something that's marvelous, like a hidden jewel you needed a push to discover. It's also likely that you'll end up less than satisfied, working on someone else's WHAT, not your own.

How Intention Works. The difference lies in owning your intention like you own your personality. As this ownership rubs off on others, they begin to become magnets for you. We all get things done through and with others. It's a subtle thing, the difference between intention and forcing, and the way other people get drawn in. But having the intention of working in your WHAT-WHERE-WHO arena is like leaving a breadcrumb trail for others to follow. When people feel your enthusiasm and your focus, they become interested in where you're headed, and start opening doors that even they might not otherwise have seen.

My first job after grad school benefited from breadcrumbs. I was about to get married, I had just moved to Texas, had a master's degree in French (thinking I was going to teach it), and a vague notion that my career was in the field of education. I needed to earn some money quickly, so I took a temporary customer service job with a credit card company. Wouldn't you know the person working next to me had an uncle who was starting an alternative school? It had a vocational training focus to get underprivileged kids off the streets and teach them workplace skills. It sounded interesting to me.

I had been convinced that I wanted to be a French teacher, but I started realizing I needed something more concrete. I found the idea of working with these kids both challenging and fascinating. I had an inkling that I would be working in my sweet spot when I started getting excited about helping people gain useful skills, so they could become productive and proud of themselves.

The next thing I knew, I was teaching in an innovative program, working with federal funding and local teachers. This path took me from working with underperforming kids, to ending up in grad school earning a PhD in adult education. From temp job to teaching, and ultimately a career in leadership training and change management consulting — quite a set of breadcrumbs! While my image of possible futures wasn't crystal clear early in my career, the intention of being a catalyst to help people change their lives was.

Was my first job the one I always wanted? No, I wasn't destined to stay in public education as a high school teacher. But spending a couple of years in this environment deepened my understanding of education and counseling. I began to sprout my wings as a spark for developing people's insight and awareness. This is where intention led me to the next job. I met an immediate need, to earn money before I got married, but kept myself open to possibilities. My temp job cubicle neighbor led me to an information interview, which landed me an innovative teaching role, which put me on my lifelong path. *Guided Drift* at work once again.

Intention capitalizes on *Guided Drift*. I pick up my anchor and let the tide do its work — but I have a compass and a general sense of a destination. Sometimes the side currents sweep me off course, but I'll only adopt the new course if it offers some aspect of my WHAT-WHERE-WHO.

Intention allows for drift, while forcing can feel like a knife severing the line to your anchor.

Can your intention change? Of course. But like your core values, it doesn't change often or easily. Intention seeps out of your WHAT-WHERE-WHO, the meaning that you want to make of your own life. Joseph Campbell says that life has no meaning, that we bring the meaning to it. I call that your intention, your WHAT-WHERE-WHO declaration.

Not Making a Decision *IS* Making a Decision

Your head can feel like a pinball machine at times like this. So many things to consider, or too few things to consider — they both get our self-talk bouncing off the walls. Whether there's too much or too little going on, it becomes easy to stop making decisions and start floating. Why? Because when our brain gets overloaded it's going to call on a stress response so that you can continue to breathe and function. A form of Freezing is to let yourself float. Float is different from *Guided Drift*. *Guided Drift* hooks into the anchor and the bearings you have created in your Past-Present-Future investigation and your WHAT-WHERE-WHO declaration. Float tempts you to let a decision make you, instead of you making the decision.

This is when not making a decision becomes a decision. It often feels easy in the moment, but you end up experiencing the consequences as a forcing. This is when the self-talk starts turning towards "I HAD to do this, I didn't have a choice, I NEEDED the job." When you start thinking and talking like that, you interpret this giving up on choosing as being forced into a decision. Now you're in that victim space, rather than being in the exciting place of co-creating your future with your new boss and teammates.

So what's a chooser to do? First — WAKE UP! See the floating for what it is — a stress response. Second, get back to paying attention. Third, take charge of the choice. Even if you choose the job you floated into and it wasn't exactly in your intention path, choose it deliberately. At this time in your life, you may need this experience — it has something to offer you.

PAY ATTENTION

Right now

What's your next move?

Remember Sean's experience at the law office? While it lacked the teamwork he craved and the opportunity to have the impact he desired, he learned a lot. First, he stuck it out for over a year. He learned to see something through its whole cycle. Second, he gained valuable knowledge on managing details and multiple projects. And lastly, he became crystal clear on what he did not want. This made the move to Denver and the new job even sweeter. He became far more intentional and determined to choose a job that filled the holes from the previous one. And he succeeded in doing just that.

Handling a Job Offer

Whether the job offer that comes first is right on your WHAT or not, it's great to be wanted! It's so seductive to be asked to the dance. Enjoy that moment! Tell people; bask in your glory — a mountain peak bagged. Then after you've enjoyed the vista and the exhilaration of getting an offer, take a good seat and think about what you have in your hand.

Before you even go through the process of actually making the decision, be sure you understand the offer. First, get it in writing. Second, if you have questions, be sure to ask them. You want to go into this with your eyes wide open. There will be enough things about the job that you won't understand until you get there. Answer what you can now.

In the next activity, I'll lead you through one way to open this kind of conversation with your prospective new boss. (If you have no more questions, skip to the section titled *Making Your Choice* on page 166.) I know this is a nerve-wracking kind of conversation, because you are balancing interest with inquiry. Keep in mind that the more you clarify now, the less likely you will feel doubtful about any part of your decision. The point is to own this decision — both its advantages and its disadvantages. Because never forget that once you make the decision, you can always make the decision right.

Activity 38

Understanding Your Offer

GO

Engage in a positive conversation with your prospective boss about clarifying your job offer.

STEPS

1. **Prepare for the conversation** by listing the items that need clarification, and what your question or concern is:

Item	Question	Item	Question
Job tasks		*PTO (paid time off)*	
Boss(es)		*Reviews*	
Pay		*Promotions*	
Other		*Other*	

2. **Practice your conversation** with a friend, or in front of a mirror — especially if you get nervous. Here are a couple of possible options on how to open the conversation:

   "Hi Bill, this is Susan. Thank you for sending me the offer so promptly. I've read through it, and I have a couple of things I want to make sure I understand. First, can we talk about the job responsibilities? Based on our previous conversation, I believe I have a general idea of the role, but could you address a couple of questions?" Proceed to ask, or you may just want to have him review the job again, and ask specific questions as issues come up, like this: "I would appreciate it if you would go over the major tasks I'll be doing, and how you see me spending most of my time."

3. **If you have a specific question, face it head on.** Pay is a good example. WARNING! Remember this is a clarification discussion, NOT a negotiation. DO NOT let yourself get into a negotiation here. And remember to go softly. First, you want to see what your potential employer's policies are.

Here goes: *"Bill, I have a question about the starting pay. It's somewhat less than I was hoping for. Could you please give me some idea about how the pay scales work there, what the review process is like, and how and when there might be an opportunity for a raise?"*

I know this may sound direct, but as long as you are polite, and remain excited about the opportunity, you will be fine. And if there is some anxiety — well then, you have clarified some more things about this job. Just make sure the concern is about the salary and not your approach.

Remember, the dollar amount is not the only deciding factor in a job. If you sense this employer is being fair, and there is room to grow, this could trump the starting salary blues. If your gut tells you this is an employer trying to get someone on the cheap, listen to that as well.

4. **Practice before you call.** And above all — NEVER handle this kind of stuff via e-mail. In fact, if it's easy to go in person, do that. This is the kind of communication that can go south very quickly over e-mail — because there is no way for your employer to hear your tone of voice or the intention to get information and clarity.

5. **Make notes about what you heard.** Be specific and detailed enough so that these notes will help you in the next step when you decide to either make the choice or negotiate.

   NOTES:

6. **How are you feeling at the end of this conversation?**

Before you undertake a negotiation, work your way through the decision itself — Activity 39, below. Once you've considered all the elements of the choice, and whether you want to go after the opportunity, then you can consider negotiation tactics, if appropriate. The strategy on negotiating — in the *Resource Center*, page 220 — will help you with the negotiating process.

Making Your Choice. The next activity poses the questions from the beginning of this chapter, and a few more. It helps you put on paper the elements of the choice you are making. Remember, no choice is perfect. As my friend and mentor Homer Coker used to say — first best is too expensive, second best comes too late, third best is good enough. But keep in mind that good enough is not compromising your gut instinct about what is good — it means balancing your intention and your desires with what can move you towards your calling right now. It's the best way I know to fight off the urge to wait around for perfection. Progress is a much better deal.

Activity 39

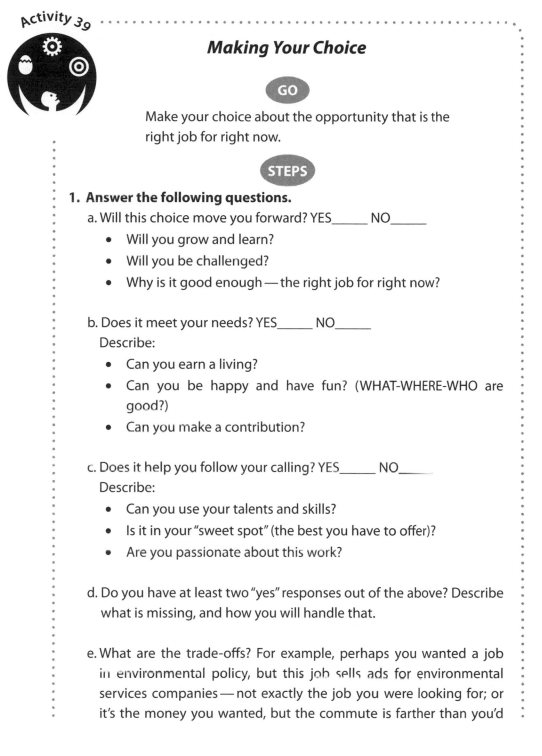

Making Your Choice

GO

Make your choice about the opportunity that is the right job for right now.

STEPS

1. **Answer the following questions.**

    a. Will this choice move you forward? YES_____ NO_____

    - Will you grow and learn?
    - Will you be challenged?
    - Why is it good enough — the right job for right now?

    b. Does it meet your needs? YES_____ NO_____
    Describe:

    - Can you earn a living?
    - Can you be happy and have fun? (WHAT-WHERE-WHO are good?)
    - Can you make a contribution?

    c. Does it help you follow your calling? YES_____ NO_____
    Describe:

    - Can you use your talents and skills?
    - Is it in your "sweet spot" (the best you have to offer)?
    - Are you passionate about this work?

    d. Do you have at least two "yes" responses out of the above? Describe what is missing, and how you will handle that.

    e. What are the trade-offs? For example, perhaps you wanted a job in environmental policy, but this job sells ads for environmental services companies — not exactly the job you were looking for; or it's the money you wanted, but the commute is farther than you'd like. List everything from the sublime to the ridiculous. I'll start you with a list of possibilities, then you finish it with the particulars of your situation.

Issue	Comments
Nature of the work	
Make a difference	
Type of company	
Boss(es)	
Co-workers	
Growth opportunity	
Pay	
Commitment/hours	
Location	
Other	

2. **Explain the deliberate choice you are making and why.**

Taking the Right Step for Right now

PAY ATTENTION

Deliberate choice

What's your next move?

Making a conscious decision is a major accomplishment. Before you call to accept the job, take a moment to experience your choice. Think about what you love about this choice, how it puts you one step further in the pursuit of your WHAT-WHERE-WHO, and how you are willing to accept the realities of this job—both the high points and the less attractive points. Be prepared to embrace the whole thing—it's part of the adventure and the learning. And remember to express your appreciation for this opportunity.

Before you have this conversation, consider both your needs and the employer's needs. A common issue will be start date. But there may be additional considerations, like relocation, completing forms, training, or certifications. Know what you need, but be flexible and ready to work out the details so your employer can feel good about them. Your next task is to take the job!

Bring It In. You are at an important crossing point. You have made a choice, and your life is about to change. If you turned down the job, you have some terrific experience in managing the job offer process, and you are diving back into your network and the process. If you took the job, then change is swirling around you!

Among the changes you face will be schedule change, people you interact with, making and managing new relationships, learning a new culture, dealing with a new boss, time constraints, fitting in time for exercise, and balancing your personal life and relationships with your new job. So, it's not crazy to feel a little crazy during this time of change.

Remember those neurons that have to pick up and move themselves? Well, they're working really hard at a time like this, and it all takes energy. So be good to yourself. Get plenty of fresh air and exercise, plenty of rest, and attend to your loved ones. That's a pretty tall order — but think balance. Like a high wire artist, you may need some tools that become your balance beam through this transition. Don't be afraid to use them! I've mentioned some of the coping tools already, and more can be found in the next chapter as you begin to settle in to your new work. If you're relocating, you will also find resources you can tap to help you with that big change, too. It's all the same stuff, with a little extra kick of adventure!

Heads Up. You're in the home stretch now. But it isn't over. Finish the stroke through thank yous and conversations, and through passing the torch. This is where we will spend a few moments anticipating your new experiences in the job, celebrate your accomplishments, and look ahead.

Settling In

You've landed. Now that the *Docking* process is underway, it's time for you to get settled in, start a new routine, and use those beginner's eyes. Since you've put so much energy into this project, this chapter simply ties the knot and secures your docking. Let's spend a few minutes taking stock, preparing for what's to come, and saying thank you to those who supported your journey.

This is an exciting time — something new to look forward to, with hopes and expectations for learning and growth. Whatever changes you have gone through to date, they were baby steps to prepare you. Now the floodgates open — change of schedule, change of people you spend your time with, and maybe even a change of address.

The Big Logistics Issues

You can manage these by setting reasonable expectations of yourself. Things roll fast at times like this — do one thing at a time, and be deliberate. Make a punch list, take a deep breath. You need to consider transportation to your job if you don't yet have a car, a place to live, a wardrobe for work, maybe even furniture if you will be moving. Write everything down and then prioritize it. Then actually work your list!

Expectations. Identify what you need to get done, as well as what you need for yourself to get through this shift. Get clear on your own needs for rest, exercise, and getting the help you need from friends and family. Sit down with them and set your expectations for the next couple of weeks, including getting them to flag you when you start to spin out of control. Focus on what is needed, and give yourself room to breathe and relax.

Money. It is tempting at a time like this to go buy a brand-new wardrobe, all the furniture you want, and that car. Pace yourself. You need to get into the job and get a sense of how it's going to work for you. You can get by on less than you think. Less is definitely more right now. Think about traveling light for a while.

Basic Preparations. Don't take on more than you have to before you start your job. What you need is a place to live (with a bed, a chair, a table and a few utensils), a way to get to work, something to wear to work, and your head on straight. Everything else is extra. Period. Don't sweat the details right now. Besides, they get in the way of the basics.

The Big Personal Issues

Handling Stress. This is an important time to pay attention to your reactions to all the things that are happening to you. It is easy to get overwhelmed with so much *to do*. It is essential to your balance to notice those moments and throw off any lopsidedness you feel. I mean things like rushing, as well as headaches and bellyaches from tensing up, and roller coaster emotions. Abiding by the expectations you set will help a lot. And lean on the people who can support you now. It's OK to ask for 100 percent help from them at a time like this. You will return the good deed in the future when they need 100 percent from you.

Emotions. Whether you wear your emotions on your sleeve or bury them in the pit of your stomach, acknowledge that they are running rampant. The cool and nonchalant approach doesn't serve you well here. Neither does the frantic chicken dance. Your hormones are running on high octane, so don't feel crazy if you need a little more rest or if you need to insist on your exercise more rigorously. You will need both — but don't flee into overdrive mode either.

Find someone to talk to, a way you can blow off steam or just hang loose — with no expectations. If you feel stuck on any issue or really frustrated, consult those sections in the *Resource Center* (*Stuck* is 8, *Frustration* is 2). And remember, if you weren't feeling these things, then you wouldn't be in the middle of a change.

Keeping Your Eye on the Ball. No matter what pops up in the weeks before you show up for that first day of work, remember to stay focused on what is important:

PAY ATTENTION

Eye on the ball

What's your next move?

- Let your emotions serve you, not rule you

- Manage your money

- Stick to basic preparations

- Stay true to your WHAT-WHERE-WHO stand

In the New Role

The first weeks and months are going to feel like you are breaking in a new pair of shoes. Some days your feet will hurt, some days it will feel just right, and some days things will just rub you the wrong way. It takes time to find a pattern, to see how you fit, and to begin to get comfortable. Don't expect miracles the first day or the first week.

Managing Expectations. The one thing I can guarantee you is that everything will not be as you imagined it — including the things you were most sure about! Some things will be better, some will be worse, some a complete surprise. This is like imagining what it's like to live in someone else's house. However it looks when you visit, you can be sure it will be different when you live there 24/7.

Roll with the Punches. As you encounter each new challenge, work on experiencing it and paying attention — mostly to yourself and how you're handling the trials and tribulations of learning how to fit in and get your work done at the same time. Also pay attention to how they do things around there — every house has a slightly different set of cultural rules akin to whether or not it's OK to put your elbows on the table at dinner. By rolling with the punches, you'll try not to over-react when strange things happen. Respond as best you can, take an objective look at the situation, then size it up when you have the time and brainpower to understand it.

The kinds of experiences may range from how people act in meetings — from quiet to noisy and opinionated, to how people interact with bosses and team members — from military discipline to hanging with best buds. It includes e-mail and phone protocol, and when, where, and how you take lunch. And it especially includes how people manage time — late or on time for meetings? Common start time, or people roll in whenever? You get the picture. This is the stuff of getting in the groove of the place and the people.

The Water Cooler Phenomenon. After a couple of months you may begin to think you understand the job, and you start forming some opinions that shape your experience there. Try not to buy in to the gossip chain. Assess the situations, the people, and the work requirements against your own needs and interests. Hallway talk can be both the lifeblood of an organization and its poison. As you pay attention to your needs, and what you can do for the organization, keep paying attention to what matters.

Managing Relationships. This is a biggie, but let's at least cover some key points. Your ability to manage your relationships with your bosses, your peers, and your reports will make or break the work experience. This is no different from managing relationships in your family. You learned well growing up — who's in charge, who has influence, who you can push around, and how to get your way. You want to pick up all the good lessons you learned there and apply them on the job. Naturally, though, you want to avoid pushing people around and getting your way unless it's about influencing and making good things happen.

What's different from your family is that these people don't have to love you no matter what. And now you're learning to balance the worlds of collaboration and competition at a higher level. Of course, you've been doing this all your life — whether it was with siblings, playmates or teammates. And just like then, you want to play for win/win. You want to make happen what is in both your own best interest *and* the best interest of your group and your company. That can be a tall order!

So manage your relationships. In particular, learn from day one to manage your boss. I don't mean push her around. I mean learn her strengths and limitations, what language she speaks (is she into numbers and logic or ideas and collaboration?), and how to bring out the best in her. If you can do it with your siblings and teammates, you can do it at work. Keep working the win/win.

Managing relationships doesn't mean over-thinking them. It goes right back to paying attention. You want to roll with the experiences, *and* apply your ability to notice what's going on and respond appropriately. Above all, use your common sense. If that's not your strong point then find a teammate who prides herself on practicality and learn from her. The other part of managing relationships is finding people to work with who complement your abilities. We don't get anything meaningful done alone — so hitch your wagon to people who complement your abilities and work will be even more fun.

You want to make a difference. My friend Barry Oshry defines empowerment as making happen what you want to make happen, and what the

PAY ATTENTION
Common sense

What's your next move?

organization needs to have happen. Think about it. If I'm in my family, or community, or work and I get to do what I want to do while meeting their needs — that is power. Look for those crossing points. As you pay attention to your environment you will begin to learn the signals. They range from collaborating with a teammate, to taking on a project lead role, to ignoring the gossip and doing what you think is right.

This notion of making happen what you want to make happen means engaging three elements — thinking about strong outcomes, feeling confident and secure about what you have to contribute, and acting on what you want to make happen. Keep your gut instinct — what your heart is telling you — front and center. Your heart is faster than your brain. So when you can sync them all together — heart, head, and action — you are indeed making happen what you want to have happen, and what the situation calls for. You are becoming an influencer.

People have written libraries about managing relationships at work. While there's some good stuff out there, in the beginning, trust your instincts and stick to these basic guidelines:

Tips for Staying on Your Game with Co-worker Relationships

- Manage your boss

- Find people who complement your abilities

- Focus on respect and collaboration

- Find your ethical and moral compass

- Make happen what's best for both you and the company

When Problems Crop Up. There will be moments when the job feels like it's going south. Your self-talk starts kicking in: "This isn't what I signed up for; this place is screwed up; I can't work like this." Hang on for a while. Every job has its high spots and low spots. Why do you think we compared this to a glacier climb? Sometimes it's downright cold out there, and tough. Get yourself to a plateau, take a good seat, and think through where you are. And remember, you have mentors and other supporters out there to help. We all need a little help from time to time. Even if the job is 95 percent terrific, you will run into snags.

What If I *Really* Don't Like It? It's always something of a crapshoot — joining a new company and a new team. If you've been at it a couple of months and getting out of bed in the morning is something like crawling into a bear cave in the middle of winter — dark, dank and anxious about an attack — then you may need to examine what's up.

Quit or Stay? When it's that ugly, it feels like we need to hightail it out of there — after all, it doesn't feel safe, and the stress of imminent attack will wear out even the most enthusiastic among us. But before you make the decision to quit, figure out what is going on that is really driving you away.

Outside of imminent physical and psychological damage, the job not working out deserves some analysis before you walk away. Sometimes you need to get over the hump. Do you remember what your parents said about joining a team when you were a kid? I always told my kids that they needed to finish what they started. That meant that if baseball season was eight weeks, and at week two they wanted to quit — they had to gut it out, because they made a commitment to ten other kids and a coach.

Give It a Fair Shot. Look at your situation the same way. Do your best to give it six months, preferably a year. In the greater scheme of things, it's a worthwhile commitment. Even when the job is not a good match, it has something to teach you. Perhaps it is learning to be patient, perhaps it is coming to understand why you really don't like this kind of work or this kind of company. One of my favorite quotes is from novelist Zora Neale Hurston, who once said, "There are years that ask questions, and years that answer." A year unfolds answers in ways you cannot even imagine right now. Give it enough of a run to understand it, and learn what you are running towards, not what you are running away from. Always towards. This way when you pick up and move you have a vision of what else is possible for you now, rather than a hole you need to fill.

So if you think you might want to quit, consider the following:

Tips for Deciding When and Whether to Go

- Stay long enough to understand a full cycle of work

- Find out what you do like and what you don't like

- Be willing to push through the challenges

- Learn more about what you want so you can move toward it

What If I *Really* Love It? This might seem like a silly thing to call out, but it's so important! It is so likely that you will love your new job, because you have done the homework to find a good fit. So revel in it, bask in the fun, the learning, the new friends, the sense of accomplishment, and the appreciation you are shown for doing a good job.

Your biggest challenge now is to keep finding the challenges and to manage the change as it comes upon you. This keeps the job exciting — even if it brings some stress along the way.

Mostly, feel good about loving your job. Share your enthusiasm with your friends, whether they are having a good time too or not. Don't be afraid to share your excitement — you may help others see what is possible for them. Think of what philosopher Marianne Williamson says: "Your playing small does not serve the world."

Your fun and excitement can become a teaching time for you as well. You can help others see how very possible it is to do what they love. So spread the word, dig in, and relish it like a bite of your favorite popsicle on a hot summer day.

Passing on the Torch. As you finish this process and begin the next opportunity, you can now become a mentor yourself. You have a great experience set — you've worked with mentors, you've done some self-discovery — now you're ready to help someone else. I'm not asking you to do this just as a good citizen (although that in itself is a fine reason) — but I'm asking you to do it because something happens when we teach others. We solidify what we have learned, we become firmer in what we are committed to learning for ourselves, and we feel energized by working with others.

A great example in my life is the marriage-preparation work my husband and I chose to volunteer for when we were married about twelve years. Our church prepares young couples about to marry with a one-day workshop. We do this because we want to give back to our community, but we also know that it builds and maintains our marriage relationship and it keeps us closely connected to other people who believe as strongly as we do in marriage. By surrounding ourselves with people who believe and practice the same values we hold, we become re-energized and committed to developing our own relationship skills.

This principle applies to many things you do in life. Surround yourself with people who want to learn and grow like you do. Become a mentor so you can get refreshed on what you love about what you contribute to the world. Pass on the torch — get involved in someone else's experience and help them discover their WHAT-WHERE-WHO of life.

Tying up Loose Ends. You may have a few other loose ends you want to tie up. If you want to keep a journal of your experience, you can make some final notes on your Project Plan, organize your papers from the search, and file them away. I guarantee you this will be great fun to open twenty years from now. It may even help you coach your own children, or other young seekers someday!

Another possibility may involve an interview you had along the way that particularly intrigued you. Often we meet people and run into opportunities that we're not ready for yet, but that hold the seed of a future role. It's always a good idea to reach out to such people and let them know about the job you've accepted. This gives you the chance to place a marker out there. You can ask if you might contact them again in the future, when you have more experience. People rarely say no, since this could be the spark of a future working relationship that could make their life easier and set your career on fire!

These are small steps. But they do take some energy and deliberate time allocation. Yet these are the kinds of actions that pull you into your futures. Put it on your calendar to follow through — you won't regret the time you put in.

Gratitude

You've landed the opportunity and you're ready to move on to the next phase of your life! Amazing — don't you feel good about yourself?

At this point, it's time to express your gratitude to those who helped you, and maintain your relationships by telling people where you are docking. This is about both etiquette and gratitude. When you tell people who were involved with your search where you ended up, you get two things done.

1. They appreciate that you took the time to update them.
2. You create the occasion to express your gratitude for their help.

This keeps your relationship in forward momentum. And you're doing the right thing.

Your mentor deserves special attention. Do a recap with her. Tell her about the job. As you thank her, explain how she helped you. You can keep this relationship moving forward as well by asking for her input on how to keep learning in your new job. Find a special way to show your gratitude to those who made a special effort to be there for you — whether through a final note of appreciation, or something more personal, either a thoughtful (but not expensive) gift, or offer your services in assisting them with a Pet Project. Perhaps a gift certificate to a favorite restaurant or the coffee shop where you met, a houseplant or flowers, movie tickets, or time helping in her garden would be appropriate.

You have so much to be thankful for, and it's important to acknowledge what others have given you. Don't forget to take time to celebrate with them — they want it as much as you do. Just a coffee or a beer, with all its camaraderie, will do the trick.

Next Stop? Simply What, Where and Who

I am so excited for you. You have pinpointed a WHAT in your life and identified the WHO and WHERE elements that allow you to live a fuller, purposeful life. You have taken the time, the energy, and the courage to examine your past, your present and your possible futures. You have successfully launched a new adventure in your life. It's as simple as becoming the shapers of our own lives versus sliding into the role of victims, vulnerable to any storm that can take us off course.

You are now a shaper. You have made choices successfully and you will continue to make them. Don't ever forget that you make the decision, then you make the decision right. You have made this choice, and while you are certain to run into some bumps in the road, you have these new skills at your fingertips. You can revisit just a page or a section of the book from time to time. And don't forget to take advantage of the guidance and the helping hand at the Web site www.ChooseOnPurpose.com.

In the end, it is the simplest questions that are the most profound. Answering the simple questions matters the most: What do I want to do next? What draws on my skills and talents, gives me something to do, and contributes to the world?

As we part ways for now, I just want to remind you of my favorite saying: Follow your bliss! Doors will open. You do that by engaging in that wonderful experience of *Guided Drift*.

You guided yourself here by uncovering possibilities and determining options so you could, indeed, choose on purpose. You are willing to have a foot in both worlds of drift and guidance, and allow yourself to be open enough for what life will deliver you. It is a cycle you can now repeat as you reach each plateau of your life and begin to create your next new beginning.

You know so much more now about who you are and what you have to offer the world! The collaboration of our energies in this process stirs up even more potential to make happen what we want to have happen, and what the world around us needs to have happen. Life is a series of good enoughs marching towards progress. You keep the march lively by asking the questions that help you continually develop work you love, people you want by your side, and places you can grow. Keep choosing what you love, so you can love what you do.

RESOURCE CENTER

Getting Things Done

A real-world guide to get out there and make things happen, based on experience in over 200 organizations.

Contents

Picture Work You Love

What You'll Find

How to Find the Crossing Point between Your Talents and Your Passions

Nature works in fabulous ways by providing just the right abilities to the creature that needs them the most, from wide eyes for a cat's night vision, to strong legs for a wild horse. The same applies to us humans. Some of us are outfitted with strong bodies to dance or fight fires, and some of us are endowed with artistic hands for the piano or the canvas, or brains for rocket science. The trick is in knowing our bodies and minds well enough to discern how to apply these abilities to our work in this world. Knowing what you want isn't always so straightforward.

Your calling is where you have the most fun, where you feel the most turned on and in tune with yourself. If you're drawing a blank, think about anything you've done in school, hobbies, part-time jobs, volunteer work or family time. Think about your dreams and who you look up to. Somewhere in those crossing points are keys to your future. The most important part is drawing on something that you're good at. This is where your confidence is up, you know you can nail it, and even if it's challenging, you're willing to give it a try.

When starting this discovery process, people end up struggling at either end of the spectrum — they either can't think of *anything* they feel good at, or they see lots of things they're good at and can't decide which one they feel most passionate about. Don't get too concerned at this point, because Phase II, *Discovery*, (starting on page 65) will help you uncover more of that. But in order to take a stab at the *Coffee House Blueprint* (page 21), the steps below may help you begin to think about something to start with in the three columns of the worksheet.

A Simple Way to Picture Work You Love

Keep in mind that your work lies at the crossing point of your passions and your potential impact on the world. It's where you make a difference to others and to yourself. So let's simplify the work world for a moment. Rather than looking at the world as a boatload of choices that will take a lifetime to wade through, let's create major buckets of interests and abilities to contemplate.

Step 1: Four Major Areas. We all have a little bit of all kinds of abilities, and when put to the test, we can perform. However, what makes us happy and fulfilled for long periods of time tends to be the stuff we are good at and which allows us to make our visible impact on the world. So even though we are many-faceted, we work best when we contribute our best ability to the right kind of work.

Keep one thing in mind as you Picture Work You Love — you can do things in each of the four areas, and any job you do will call on some amount of each. But, you will thrive in one area, most likely the crossing point between two interests and abilities.

So let's start with just four major areas. Take this one step at a time, like you're building a Lego house — start with the outside framing and work in.

Strategy: Get the Big Picture

Examine the four areas below and make some notes:

1. Based on seeing these four words, which one are you most drawn to when you think of the kinds of things you'd like to be doing on a daily basis?

2. Is there a second that also draws you in?

3. Now add some descriptors of your own to each word, and ideas of the kinds of work that might interest you.

4. Make your notes next to the boxes.

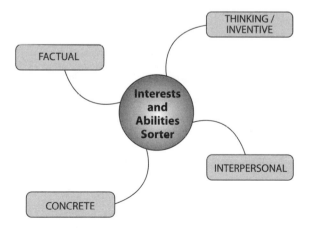

5. As we build the framework of your interests, look below at the kinds of things people do when they choose their work and their calling together. After you've examined the model on the previous page, come back and rank order the following:

Four Major Areas and What People Do

_____ Work with data and numbers (Factual)

_____ Work with your hands (Concrete)

_____ Work with people (Interpersonal)

_____ Work with ideas and designs (Thinking/Inventive)

Consider the crossing point of two areas above that might combine to make a great work arena for you.

6. Make some notes in the diagram: What do you picture yourself doing in this area?

My friend Janis is an example of these crossing points. She has been artistic all her life. She put her talents to great use early in her career as a children's clothing designer. Today, she is a jewelry designer. Same skills, abilities and passions — different kinds of work.

Notice, too, that for Janis to perform her magic, she actually taps into two sides of her brain — the concrete and the thinking/inventive. Like most of us, Janis succeeds by continually improving a couple of innate talents. So, while we're hard-wired to use our whole brains, since we can't do everything, we tend to specialize our abilities.

These whole brain concepts, developed by Ned Herrmann, provide the foundation for this easy way of picturing yourself at work. A whole brain view of ourselves recognizes that each of us has the ability to be analytical, organized, interpersonal and inventive thinkers — and — that in order to flourish, we will specialize in our finest talents.

Here's the next step in framing your work.

Strategy: Picture Yourself at Work

Look at the expanded image of interests and abilities below and answer the questions that follow it.

Attributes and Traits of Each Interest and Abilities Area

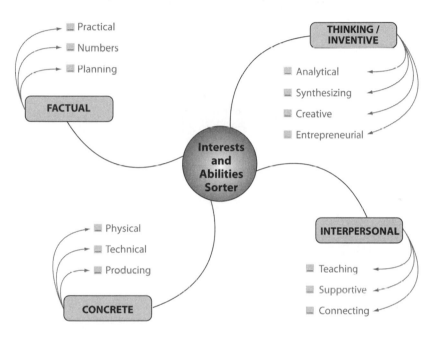

1. Identify one or two of the four gray major areas that you and others would identify as your Interests and Abilities. Star or circle them.

2. Rank order in the space before the descriptors above (1 is highest, 13 is least) to see more clearly which combinations appeal to you.

3. What other adjectives would you use to describe how you could contribute your abilities to your next job?

4. Write down your top four descriptors. What do you think?

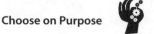

Step 2: Impact of Your Interests and Abilities. Now, let's look at the four major areas with examples of the kinds of results people produce when they work in that area. After all, this is all about the contribution you have to make.

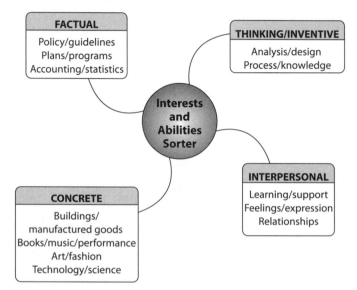

Strategy: Identify Your Impact

1. Make a few notes in the diagram about the kind of impact you want to have on the world and the results you want to create.

2. When people think of you, what do they see you doing (using the words above)?

3. What two kinds of outcomes do you see yourself contributing to the world?

4. Who will benefit from your Interests and Abilities?

Step 3: Possible Jobs in Those Areas. I have identified a few job types in each quadrant. They combine attributes of at least two adjacent interest areas. Education, for example, draws intensely on thinking and interpersonal skills.

Keep in mind that all work has elements of each of the four interest areas. This is simply a way to show you some patterns of thinking you will likely use in these kinds of careers. These are very general buckets — use them as a starting point.

Strategy: See the Setting

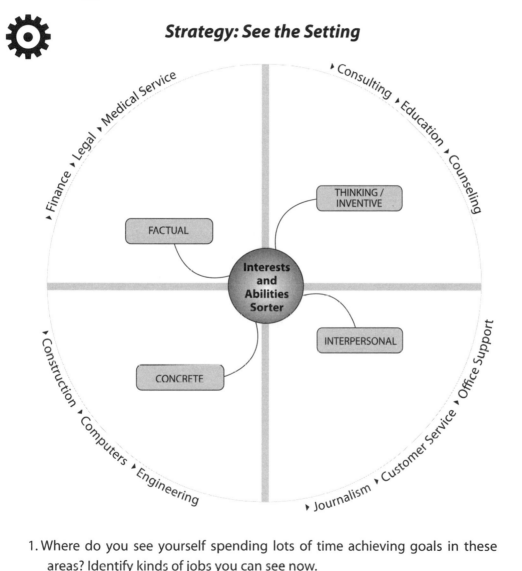

1. Where do you see yourself spending lots of time achieving goals in these areas? Identify kinds of jobs you can see now.

2. What's fun about it for you?

3. What is it about this stuff that makes you feel good about yourself?

What to Do If the Work You Love Still Isn't Popping Up

First, take a deep breath and be patient. Open up some space to listen to your heart. Go back to the simple image of Interests and Abilities on page 191.

Strategy: Trust Your Intuition

1. What questions remain?

2. What does your intuition tell you?

Second, let these ideas sink in and don't rush how they process through your system.

Third, go back to the *Coffee House Blueprint* (page 21) and complete it as best you can for now. There is plenty of opportunity to think more thoroughly about this in the *Discovery* stage. The more open you are, the more likely the focus will come.

Last, if you are already thinking that you will need more help, you may want to skip forward to Section 5 of the *Resource Center: WHAT-WHERE-WHO Now?*

But don't forget one important thing. Get out there and talk to people, try things out and experiment. You can create groundbreaking conversations that will bring ahas! to you. See Chapter 6: *Choosing*. That will teach you more than lengthy introspection. Too much thinking can be an escape from just getting on with it. So given the choice between pondering and moving, I vote for getting out — with anything from groundbreaking conversations to barista or volunteer work.

Frustration 101

What You'll Find

Understanding Frustration

Here is my favorite definition of frustration, from friend and mentor Barry Oshry:

Not making happen what you want to make happen.

This is a deceptively simple statement, with a lot of punch. Think about the last time you said, "I am SO frustrated!" I guarantee it is the result of something that just occurred that did not meet your needs or desires — from the dog not coming when you called to someone not returning your phone call. We tend to curse, stomp our feet, brood or find refuge in the fridge. We get that feeling of giving in and giving up. It's a normal human response.

These kinds of behaviors indicate our sense of powerlessness in a situation. That's what Oshry is saying — admitting frustration is admitting you are not making something happen that you want. Frustration is all about power, or actually, the lack of it — resulting in your crying out to the world "I'm frustrated!"

Once you understand that frustration is about your own power, then you can begin to do something about it — something more than the typical powerless responses of brooding or foot stomping. Dealing with your own power does not always mean taking immediate action. Above all, it means stepping back to understand

- that you are frustrated;
- what is going on; and
- what you might do about it, including nothing.

Becoming aware of your frustration is the most important first step. Without it, you begin reacting, probably emotionally and without intent or focus on what is the best result you can hope to obtain. So let's look at coping skills that will turn your frustration into meaningful outcomes.

Coping Skills for Frustration

The core coping skill for frustration is to tap into your power. Simple to say, not so easy to do when you're feeling ticked off, rejected, hassled, fidgety or otherwise distressed. This is why frustration often gets the best of us — we give in to the emotion rather than using it as a bridge to creating a better situation for ourselves.

Since we're talking about power, be clear that this will require energy from you to make it work. This energy feeds your empowerment to make positive things happen. Oshry has some ideas about power. He has spent his life investigating individual power and power in groups. Besides articulating what frustration is all about, he has helped people understand how to take action in otherwise seemingly hopeless situations.

To paraphrase Oshry's fundamental notion of empowerment, it is:

Making happen what you want to have happen and what the situation and people around you need to have happen.

When you're creating a new life — like you're doing now — this could mean finding work where you get to use your talents, in just the place where your new employer needs them. On the way to getting there, it could mean focusing your energy on creating the opportunities for contacts and interviews, rather than wasting your energy on the stuff that's not working (like being frustrated).

He adds to this notion that the effective use of power is most striking when you see people persist even when the evidence and the situation indicate that there is no power to have, or it feels useless to keep going. This is like hearing that you don't have the right degree, you live in the wrong area, no one is hiring — and you keep at it anyway. He says to keep going despite the odds, by tapping into some universal skills we all have available to us.

Tapping into Universal Skills. These available, but often unused skills include:

Take responsibility and do what you can do.
Take charge of yourself. It's OK to slump around some when things don't go your way. But don't let yourself slide into stagnation or bitterness. If you can't get a key contact to return your call, create a plan. This can include finding others that know him to help you out, or putting your energy on another contact entirely.

The main point is to move — but not randomly — with intention on something that will make what you want to have happen, actually happen.

Be self-reliant — don't get knocked around by other people's opinions.
This is a really gritty thing to do. When we are frustrated, and things aren't going the way we want them to, we all have a tendency to fall back and see what's working for other people. We become vulnerable to other people's

opinions. But look around you. The greatest strides are taken by people who don't listen to the opinions of others — those who forge their own paths. From Steve Jobs to Oprah Winfrey, examples abound of people who — against the odds — dug deep in their own souls to find the power to make happen what they wanted to make happen and what others around them needed.

This is challenging stuff. You need your energy to have the guts to strike out on your own — whether it be heading for a far off place to start afresh, becoming a troubadour musician or finishing your degree.

Make a project rather than be victim to circumstances.

As Oshry often reminds us in *Seeing Systems,* it's oh so easy to be a victim of circumstances. We just love to talk about what "they" did to us — that includes everybody from your boss to your parents, and from the rude people who won't return your calls to the bad service at the copy center when your resume looks crappy.

So we can stand on the outside, judge the others, and have, well, our nasty judgment and our resentment to show for it. Or we can jump in and do something about it. This includes doing things like changing the way we respond to bosses, parents and rude people. It even means learning how to give good feedback so we get better service without ticking off the people who are taking care of us at the copy center. Wow. Is that really possible?

It is if you're willing to ask, "What else is possible?" and create a project to change the circumstances. Again, this takes energy — but it's certainly worth it if you don't want to be mucking around in frustration anymore. The choice is yours — spend your energy being angry, or spend it building a project to get what you want and what the situation needs.

Before you take action, don't just do something, stand there.

Don't just jump into action without the old "stop, look and listen" adage playing out. What are you frustrated about — REALLY? Most of the time it's not just the situation right in front of you, but what it represents. For instance, I might be frustrated my boss won't let me fix a problem, but underneath that, I'm very frustrated that he doesn't trust me. So rather than jumping on a reaction, step back and stand there for a moment.

Consider next steps that help you:

- Take a time-out to understand what is going on
- Do what you can — no heroic moves necessary
- Focus on what you think will work for you, and no one else
- Keep yourself out of the muck of "victimhood" and into a small project with a target

This is the difference between blaming yourself for being ten pounds overweight and beating yourself up, versus going for a walk today and eating well today. This translates for you, as you find work you love, into these kinds of possibilities:

- When your contact doesn't return your call, you either find a compelling reason to call him, find someone else who knows him to find out what's going on, or focus your energy on a new lead.
- When the interview goes poorly, you can identify what you did well and focus on doing more of that, ask for feedback, or entertain the idea that you aren't looking at the right kind of work for you.

Obviously, these aren't all the choices, but some examples of where to start. What's important is thoughtfully moving forward and taking on a project. You don't want to be a casualty of another life incident, but instead an actor, doing what you can, making something happen.

So, looking at a current frustration you are dealing with, take some notes:

 ### *Strategy: Deal with Your Current Frustration*

1. What are you trying to make happen?
2. What isn't happening and why?
3. What can you affect?
4. What can't you affect?
5. What can you do now, knowing this?

Understanding and Handling Disappointment

You feel disappointed when your hopes or expectations go unfulfilled. You hoped an interview would go well, and it didn't — expectations unfulfilled. Sometimes they are unfulfilled because of your own actions or expectations, and sometimes they go unfulfilled because of things totally out of your control. Regardless, disappointment leaves you feeling as empty as frustration, and often in the same predicament of wasting energy.

We all feel disappointed from time to time. Like any emotion, though, we can work through it and find the opportunity that lies behind the cloud. The first step to coping with disappointment is to understand what is making us feel disappointed.

Disappointment comes in two forms — others disappoint us, or we disappoint ourselves. There are three keys to handling disappointment:

- Understand it
- Get clear on what you want that's different
- Identify what you can influence

Understand disappointment. When you are disappointed, debrief yourself on what happened. Find a recent or current situation and:

Strategy: Debrief Disappointment

1. What were your expectations?

2. Were they realistic? Why? Why not?

3. What role did you play in the disappointment?

Get clear on what you want. Disappointment means that something missed the mark in your interaction.

Strategy: Get Clear

1. What was missing?

2. Why was it missing?

3. What would fill the gap?

What you can influence. Sometimes you can fix a disappointment. For example, if you ran slower in a race than you expected, you may be able to train harder next time. But sometimes, the answer to alleviating your disappointment is to change the demands you make on yourself. I may decide that participating in the race is good enough for me, and I take an enormous amount of pressure off myself.

Sometimes the outcome isn't up to you all by yourself. Disappointment may come because someone else did not perform to your expectations, and you're not likely to change that anytime soon, or ever. An interview may be disappointing because the person and the organization did not, and may not ever, sync up with your needs. Even if you were excited about the opportunity, there's no point in beating yourself up over something you can't change. Deal with what you can deal with, and leave the rest alone.

So, if the answer to the question

What can you change or influence?

is nothing, walk away and move on to something you can affect. I know it sounds simple, and it's not so easy to do. But the quicker you admit what's in your scope to influence, the faster you'll be tapping into your power zone and being effective — and happy. At this point the most important thing you can do is influence your own thinking and attitude — and that is BIG!

There is little difference between handling disappointment and frustration. Both are about dashed expectations, and both can make you annoyed and sad. Over the last few years as I've read and researched about power

and change, I've run into a sage old saying a number of times. I'm not sure exactly where it comes from, and since I've seen it in several texts, it may actually come from a variety of sources, speaking to the same sense of inner power. It goes like this:

In my world, nothing ever goes wrong.

That sounds like an incredibly bold statement. Almost arrogant. But, as I've seen it explained, it is far from that. This statement doesn't say that I don't make mistakes, that I never experience failure, or being stupid or absentminded. It does, however, indicate a willingness to learn and grow from everything that happens. It also means that I won't let disappointment or frustration get the best of me — I may get bummed out for a while, or ticked off occasionally, but I see the seed of hope — eventually!

As you learn to see that nothing ever goes wrong in your world, you will get better and better at beating frustration and disappointment — simply by putting these coping skills into play:

breathe, acknowledge, act.

When things don't go the way you want them to, with this approach you begin processing things differently. You can push through the denial and the anger more quickly by asking, "What is the lesson, the opportunity for me here?" I heard someone on the radio say the "O" for obstacle hides behind it the "O" for opportunity.

I'm not trying to gloss over the fact that bad things happen. But to quote ED Hose, my illustration consultant,

When life hands you lemmings, make 'lemming-aide'!

In other words — don't just blindly jump off the cliff like that old lemming. Instead turn it around and help yourself move on to the next best thing for you.

Job Search Stuff

What You'll Find

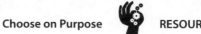

Search Stuff 101

There are some staples you need in your search tools pantry. The items, printed on good paper, include:

- Clean, simple, one page resume
- Outline for a cover letter that you can easily customize
- Work samples or portfolio, if required for your field
- References list
- Optional: business card with name, address, phone, e-mail

PLUS —

- Calendar that you can carry with you at all times

I'll talk in more detail below about resumes and cover letters. The idea of a business card is that of convenience and preparedness. If you use one, keep it very simple — your name in bold letters, with your address, phone number and e-mail address. I don't suggest you put any marketing material on it — that's what a resume is for. These are nice to have in case you need to give someone your information quickly. It makes you look organized and prepared. You can either print them up yourself using the special card stock you can buy at your local office supply store, or have them printed — they should be relatively inexpensive for a simple black and white option.

The portfolio speaks for itself. If you are in a field such as architecture, design or art then you should be well versed in putting together a portfolio. If you are a writer, be prepared to have a few samples of your work on hand as well.

The last item is a list of references. Preferably these are people you have worked for, whether as a volunteer or for pay. They will vouch for your experience and skill set. Don't forget to contact them in advance and ask their permission to use their names.

The additional item is your calendar. Never leave home without it. This is your lifeblood during a time like this, and you want to be prepared to add a contact or an interview whenever and wherever. If your calendar is not on your phone, then buy a pocket calendar you can keep on your person all the time. This will save your butt, I guarantee it!

Example of a Good, Basic Resume

Much has been written about resume writing, and I'm not going to rehash it here. Instead, I'm going to focus you on one example only. Resumes are like personalities; they come in all shapes and sizes. That said, don't get too fussy about your resume, with a couple of exceptions:

- Keep it simple, clear, precise and short
- Include a skills list at the top
- One page for up to seven years experience
- Tell the truth

The example below meets all my criteria. Feel free to fiddle around with the look, but don't get fancy. While this is marketing material, flashy doesn't count here. Remember that people will read it quickly, that search engines may scan it, and that you want people to get the gist of it in just a few lines of reading. Good enough works well here!

While this must look professional, you won't get extra points for style. Think of it like soccer, a goal is a goal, whether you did it with a fancy kick or not. Clean and simple is the rule. Get this done, then get out there talking to people.

Lastly, don't forget to keep a list of references handy.

A resume example is on the next page.

Resume Example

Sean McAllen
7 Pearapple Rd.
Waterfalls, NY 12101
(c) 518.555.3323 (h) 518.555.1051
mcallens@dickinson.edu

QUALIFICATIONS
- **Research and analysis**
- **Team leadership**
- **Taking projects from innovation to implementation**

EDUCATION

Dickinson College, 2008, B.A. American Studies
Carlisle, Pennsylvania
- Fall 2006, Study abroad in Wales
- Thesis: The Hudson River PCB Story: But Whose Story is It?
- Spring 2006, Annual Speech Contest Finalist

INTERNSHIP
2007 June-Aug   **League of Conservation Voters Education Fund,**
Washington, D.C.
Researched and created reports on ballot initiatives. Created database (in Excel) of environmental activists from grassroots canvass. Maintained voter statistics for environmental voter profiles.

EXPERIENCE
2006 May-Sept   **Flying Fish Grill, Lake Martha, NY**
Server/ Waiter: Assisted management with seasonal opening/closing .

2005 June-Aug   **Leader/Facilitator of Continental Divide Trail Hiking Adventure**
Led team of peers on 400 mile/40 day hike in Montana, Idaho and Wyoming. Responsibilities included trail guiding, procurement of supplies, and facilitating team collaboration and conflict resolution.

2005-06 May   **Takundewide Resort, Lake Martha, NY**
Building & Maintenance Team: Replaced/rebuilt docks and slips. Maintained landscaping and property safety for 30 cottages.

2004 May-Aug   **Finch Pruyn Paper Company, Inc., Waterfalls, NY**
Pulp Prep Technician: Monitored and maintained chemical levels of pulp. Added pulp to Pulper. Operated forklift for loading/unloading pulp bails. Maintained, organized and cleaned paper mill.

LEADERSHIP
2004-2008   **Dickinson Varsity Lacrosse**
Four-year Letter winner
2008 Leadership & Commitment Award winner

2002-2006   **Sports Instruction**
Dickinson College Lacrosse Clinics (2003 - 2006)
Waterfalls High School Lacrosse Camps (Summer 2002-2005)

Resume Keywords and Customization

The Internet is jam-packed with advice on writing good resumes. You are free to roam, and you will find some good advice out there. But I think for the most part it's a waste of time. Not because you won't pick up a few good tips. But you can easily get stuck perfecting something, where good enough is just fine. And it gets confusing with all that input.

There are, however, two additional things to consider in writing a good resume in the twenty-first century: keywords and customization. First, while most of the time you will be handing your resume to people you talk to (often through e-mail), occasionally it will fall into the hands of a search engine, and you want to be ready. Search engines look for keywords to identify candidates. The best way to figure out the keywords is to look at ads for the kinds of jobs you want. They will lead you to language that you can put in your resume — as long as it really describes your skill set! NEVER put something in a resume that isn't true — it will come back to bite you.

Second, you should customize your resume for different kinds of careers. You may have up to two or three areas you are considering. Each area may require a slightly different emphasis in your resume. For example, Sean's outdoor experience can be applied to either environmental jobs or sports industry jobs, depending on how he describes it.

The beauty of word processing is that in an hour you can customize your resume to the requirements of a particular job. As always, be clear that your description aptly matches the skills you can bring to the organization.

Example of a Good Cover Letter

Each cover letter will be unique for the job opportunity. It is still a good idea, though, to have a boilerplate letter ready to go. Great cover letters are works of art:

- They are very short (150–175 words)
- They express your passion and excitement for the work
- They don't repeat your resume

Here is a **cover letter** that goes with the resume you just saw.

7 Pearapple Rd.
Waterfalls, NY 12101
August 17, 2008

Ms. Bess Trelluf
The Didier Group
330 Maryland Ave., N.E. Suite 506
Washington DC 20002

Dear Ms. Trelluf:

This letter responds to your need for a Public Relations Associate in your Washington, DC office. My experience ranges from working on the front line at a paper mill to analysis and report writing at the League of Conservation Voters. This combination has heightened my skill set to implement projects in environmental advocacy.

My degree in American Studies focused on environmental policy, so I possess a well-rounded understanding of the complexities of many social and environmental issues. My fervent interest and understanding of agricultural, energy and natural resource issues will enable me to enhance the impact of your company's goals.

I can hit the ground running, so I can quickly become a contributing member of the Didier Group. I offer strong skills in writing, research, communication and organization. I am highly motivated and thrive in a team atmosphere. I can turn your ideas into projects, and projects into results.

I look forward to meeting with you to further discuss my future with the Didier Group.

Sincerely yours,

Sean McAllen
Enclosure: Resume

E-mails and Internet Presence

E-mail is a very unique kind of tool. It passes information quickly, but unlike letters, does not hold the ability to suitably convey emotion. Handwriting a letter provides some permission to express feeling; typed letters express formal communication. Typed words on a screen do not do either nearly as well.

In addition, e-mails, by nature, work best when they are very short. People's e-mail boxes can contain 100 or more items in their inbox in a day. They don't read non-essentials, so short and sweet is required. But e-mails are also not excuses to use a text message approach. Use proper English, no abbreviations, and no slang.

Write these e-mails the same way you write a hard copy letter — only shorter. Use brief paragraphs of two or three sentences, and write only two to four paragraphs in total. If the e-mail is an introduction to your cover letter and resume, make it no more than two short paragraphs.

Your decision to make the e-mail the cover letter depends on your read of the person you are sending it to. If you get the feeling that keeping it easy and quick will get more attention, go for the e-mail cover letter. If you sense a need to be more formal, either e-mail to let the target employer know a hard copy resume and cover letter are coming, or attach both to a shorter e-mail.

Besides e-mail, pay attention to your online presence in general. If you have something on Facebook that touts your party animal exploits, it's time to take that down. I've read that a significant percent of employers look for online information on job candidates.

Let Facebook, MySpace and their clones work for you instead. Use it as another marketing tool. It's OK to write about your hobbies and personal interests, as well as your professional goals. But let it be a personal expression of your strengths, not your limitations.

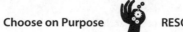

Example of a Thank You Note

The rules of writing thank you notes are simple:

- Be prompt
- Be short and sweet (80-110 words)
- Be authentic and specific
- Do it by hand

Be prompt — write the note within twenty-four hours of your meeting. There are three reasons for this — do it while it's fresh on your mind, so you won't forget, and to get it over with.

Be short and sweet — it's the thought that counts. This isn't about wowing them with your prose. It's about showing respect, appreciation for their time, and letting them know you are interested.

Be authentic and specific — speak in your own language and address something specific about the conversation you had. Smart people (the ones you want to work for) sense meaningful correspondence. Specifically addressing some aspect of your discussion shows them how closely you were paying attention. And this note becomes the attention getter for you.

Do it by hand — get a nice box of thank you stationery and use it! Nothing says personal commitment better than personal stationery. But don't use anything too flowery or goofy — keep it understated. Nor does it have to be plain, boring white — make it a reflection of you. Just keep your pen, your stamps, and the snail mail address handy.

A Basic Thank You Note

September 21, 2008

Dear Ms. Trelluf,

Thank you for the lively interview and discussion yesterday. I appreciate the time and energy you gave me to better understand your company and the role you want to fill.

I continue to have a strong interest in the job we discussed. I believe more than ever, after our conversation, that I can provide the support your department needs. I think my paper mill experience helps me bridge the idea to implementation gap, something I know is important to you.

I'm excited about the prospect of making a difference at the Didier Group. I look forward to the next steps.

Sincerely,

Sean McAllen

The Protocol of Timelines and Follow-up

There are three key things to remember about managing timelines and following up with people.

Consistency — above all, do what you say you're going to do. If you said you'd follow up in a week, then do so. This is a time to be a person of your word.

Tracking — keep good notes and put everything in your calendar. Even if you are a sticky note person and tend to be scattered, gather all your energy to keep good track of this stuff. It helps you be consistent, and to stay sane when lots of things are flying.

Patience — your timeline is not their timeline. You want them to pick up the phone TODAY — but they have other priorities on their agendas. Just stick to your consistency plan and be patient.

Regarding timing for follow-up calls and e-mails, follow these simple suggestions. Don't hound people — then you become an annoyance. But do stay consistent — I recommend you give people at least a few days to return a call or an e-mail, preferably a work week. The key, though, is to consistently follow up when you say you will, without doggedly tracking them down. You'll find the right rhythm with the different kinds of industries you encounter, so trust your instinct and stay on top of things.

Pre- and Post-Interview Activities

PRE-INTERVIEW. Interviews require some special attention. Like trying out for a play, there is research to be done, lines to learn, and some mental prepping to do.

Well before the day of the interview, do your homework on the company, the industry and the type of job you're interviewing for. You can do this online, and also by talking to people in your network, including anyone you know who may work for the company. Also review the homework you've done on yourself — your interests, what you're good at, what you love to do. Review any notes you've taken from your information interviews and your conversations with your mentor.

Give yourself a breather before you have the interview. Don't pack your day with too much stuff to do. If you can, get some exercise either the morning before the interview or the day before, depending on the time of the interview. This will help blow off some nervous steam, and get your whole body prepared to be "on."

Don't cram. Don't try to fit in your research, your exercise, figuring out what you will wear, into the few hours before the interview. It will have the same effect it did on you in school — you'll feel tired and frazzled before you get there.

When it comes to practicing your lines, this has more to do with having responses prepared for some of the standard questions you will get in an interview. You also want to be prepared to ask them some questions. The next section on improving your interview skills will go over some of those questions to ask and to answer.

Last, you have spent a lifetime preparing for this interview. Above all, be yourself and show them what you are made of — authenticity rules!

POST-INTERVIEW. If you have the time, treat yourself — whether it's to a leisurely walk, a latte, or a movie. Let the dust settle a little before you analyze what happened — keep yourself from doing the over-analysis thing.

It's always great to write down your impressions — what you liked, what you didn't like — both about your own performance, and about the job, the company and your interviewer.

- What did you learn? About yourself? About the company? About the potential match?
- How did it feel and fit? Comfy? Too tight? Too loose?
- Do you feel good about it? OK? Not sure?

Roll around in these feelings and intuitions. Once you've had some time to mull it over, connect with a good friend or mentor and talk about the experience. This is kind of like the cool down after running a race — you need an opportunity to let the gears in your body and your mind slow down.

Of course, you want to do your follow-up work within the next twenty-four hours. This includes a thank you note, as well as anything you may have committed to getting back to your interviewer — whether it is work samples or more references. Regardless of how you think it went, if you are interested in the job, follow up with a phone call in a week — it shows continued interest. The rest is in the hands of *Guided Drift*.

Improving Your Interviewing Skills. You have been spending a lot of time working on your interviewing skills if you have been doing lots of information interviews. The key to a good interview is the ability to converse, to describe yourself, and to answer questions the interviewer throws at you.

With enough information interviews under your belt, you've had this experience plenty of times. If not — get out there and get it, it's yours for the taking. I know for some of you conversation does not come easy. If you have one statement about yourself you can begin with (probably from your declaration statement) and one question to ask — that is a good enough beginning. Trust that the discussion will create itself. It's most likely the interviewer will lead you anyway — but have something in your back pocket just in case.

A second part of interviewing is preparing for a handful of questions that are often asked at interviews. They include:

- Tell me about yourself.
- Why are you interested in this job?
- Why should we hire you?
- Tell me about your greatest strength.
- Tell me about your greatest weakness.
- What do you do for fun and relaxation?

In addition to these basic questions, great interviewers will want to place you in situations where they can assess how you will behave. For example, they may describe a problem or challenge and ask you to explain how you would handle the situation. Or they might ask you to tell them about a challenge you had in a previous job and then ask probing questions to get you to describe what you actually did to resolve the problem.

So another way to prepare is to think about things you have done, how you behaved in the situation, and what you learned from it. These could all come up in an interview.

One last thing about interviewing. You want to take the opportunity to interview the company as well. You owe it to yourself to understand as much as you can about the culture, about how they do things around there.

Here are a few questions to get you started. Don't be shy about asking. If the job turns up for you, but the company makes you miserable, it won't be worth the anxiety. Like a great outfit, if it doesn't fit, and in fact if it doesn't flatter you, don't buy it.

Interviewing the Company
- What do employees say it's like to work here?
- What are the company values? How do you see those showing up on a day-to-day basis?
- If you could pick three adjectives to describe what it's like to work here, what would they be?
- What's a typical advancement path in this job? What would be next for me, and when might it happen?
- Based on your experience, what's unique about working here? What do employees like the best? And if you dare: the least?

Making the Time at the Interview Work for You.
This is also a time to pay attention to how you are treated and what the place feels like. Are people friendly? Do they look you in the eye? Was the interviewer on time and professional? How do the workspaces look and feel to you? What

do you see people doing? Is there tension in the air? Do people chat? Put your antenna on here and simply pick up the vibes.

The person who is interviewing you has a need — someone to provide a service or a product for him. This is no different than finding a librarian to help you find some information. You are lacking something; it's creating a pain in your life. Your prospective employer has a pain too — he needs someone to help him produce something. Now you have a need as well — that of wanting to find something enjoyable to do that uses your skills and talents.

You're both out to fill gaps! The interview, therefore, is a structured conversation, built to get from you enough information so employers can make a decision on whether they want to hire you. It is, however, a two-way street. Don't forget, you're looking for the right opportunity that fits you right now. This means all of you — your passions, skills, and purpose.

If you try to force your way onto the job (because you're feeling frantic to get a job) — and they're desperate to fill a job — you may land something, but it may not be a fit. You want to find enough information from them so you can use something I call an intention versus forcing thing. Your intention is to get a job where you feel you can give something and feel good about yourself. But if you force it and jam yourself into something that is not right, you'll start to feel some aches and pains, which both you and your employer will eventually share.

Pay attention — put all your senses into play to feel what is working for you. What do your eyes see? Your ears hear? Your hands feel in a handshake? What does the flip-flop of nervousness in your stomach, or that stiff neck tell you? Does it feel interesting? Exciting? Challenging? Like you can grow and learn here? Are people friendly? Or do you get that nagging feeling that something isn't right? Your body will tell you how it is responding to the situation, if you simply listen to it.

Let's look at the interview process itself, and some basic dos and don'ts before you go. I'm not a strong proponent of reading up on all the "foolproof" techniques of interviewing. When you interview you are under too much stress to remember a long list of how-tos. So stick to these three basics.

Tips on the Best Way to Interview:

1. Know yourself
Know enough about your WHAT-WHERE-WHO so you can talk about it

2. Be prepared
1) Be bold — talk about your strengths and skills
2) Be humble — talk about your limitations
3) Do your homework on the job, company and industry
4) Be ready to ask good questions
5) Feel good about yourself — rest, talk to a supporter beforehand, exercise and breathe

3. Tell the truth
There's nothing more to say about that.

If they don't choose you, even if you were crazy about the opportunity, try hard not to take it personally. I know that sounds like an impossible request. But this is where you simply have to have faith, accompanied with a dose of patience and solid resilience.

First, there are many reasons you might not have gotten the job: 1) there was an insider (someone who already worked for the company), and they were required to do some external interviews; 2) their budget was frozen and they were no longer able to hire; 3) a more qualified candidate got the job (more experience, broader skill set); 4) you didn't fit the culture. The list could go on and on, but it's enough to understand that there are many factors, some of which are out of your control. Sometimes, it's just not the right match — simple as that. You're going to the dance, and this isn't the right partner.

Chalk this up to experience. You'll be even better in the next interview. You'll have a keener sense of the kind of work environment you want to be in, you'll know yourself even more.

In the end, the interview goes both ways. Trust yourself enough to provide good answers, ask good questions, and observe the cues of the energy and the environment of this workplace.

And then — relax, have faith, and have fun.

Negotiating. Much has been written and taught about the negotiation process. This isn't a course on negotiating, but I am going to boil it down to the core. The next activity asks a handful of questions that prepare you for the process.

Strategy: Prepare for and Manage a Basic Job Offer Negotiation

1. Prepare for the negotiation by answering these questions:

a. Will you take this job regardless of the results of your negotiation? YES_____ NO_____

b. Are you prepared to turn the job down if the negotiation does not meet your needs? YES_____ NO_____

You must know what you want before you enter negotiations. Negotiate only if you need to, not just to "look tough." It lacks authenticity. If you will take the job no matter what, then this is a process to try to better your hand, but the result is not a deal breaker for you. If you know you must improve some element of the offer to make this an acceptable choice for you, then unsatisfactory results are a deal breaker for you.

2. Prepare for the conversation by practicing a respectful, cordial, yet firm approach. Remember two things here:

- Intention versus forcing — if you drive too hard a bargain you will have residual resentment to deal with. Forcing may push the relationship and the issue over the edge of reason. Your intention to create the elements of a good choice is key.

- What goes around comes around — people and relationships are universally interconnected. Maintain cordiality and respect in your negotiation — it isn't a win/lose battle — view it as a win/win dialogue. Whether you take the job or not, the result will be in the best interest of both parties.

- Consider this — if you receive better conditions, you enter the job a happy camper, poised for productivity. If you don't, then this match was not meant to be, and you can part amiably, with some experience under your belt, and the respect of the potential employer.

3. Remember to ask for help from your mentor, friends, or even just practicing in the mirror. Consider an approach like:

"Hi Bill, I am really excited about the offer. This is just the kind of work I want to sink my teeth into. (Wait for a response; if none continue.) *I do have a question I'd like to discuss with you. I was thinking the salary would be higher, given my skills and experience.* (Wait for a response. If none, again continue with one or more of these follow-up questions.)

"What are the possibilities from your point of view? Where do you think we can go from here? What else can you tell me about the job? The company?" If non-negotiable, continue: *"I understand your position. I'd like to think about this some more, and I'll get back to you by our agreed response date. Is there anything else you think might help in my decision? Thanks for your time."*

If you get the opportunity to continue the negotiation (for example, Bill says, *"What are you thinking?"*), then be prepared to be specific (and reasonable) in your request: *"I was looking for $3,000 more."* Bill may then tell you he will see what he can do. Thank him for the effort, and ask him when you might hear back. End the conversation on a high note.

From here, you will return to the key questions above — do you want this or not? Above all, keep your eye on your intention, what you value in choosing your WHAT-WHERE-WHO, and maintaining courtesy in your relationships.

If you decide to turn down the job, show an upbeat attitude and appreciation for the offer: *"Hi Bill, I really appreciate the offer and find the work you do is so interesting. At this time, however, I don't think it's a good fit for me."*

Be prepared with some good reasons, stated respectfully and positively, if he

asks you why it's not a good fit. Examples: *"A smaller (larger) company would be better for me; the job isn't exactly what I'm looking for — I realize I'm better off with more/less structure, something more focused/broader; in order to pay off my school loans, I need a little higher starting salary."* Finish on a high note: *"I hope our paths will cross again in the future. Thank you for your time and consideration."*

Don't forget to send a thank you note regardless of which way you decide.

Your practice script:

Remember: Do all this by phone or in person, and think Win/Win.

Movement

What You'll Find

What Does Movement Have to Do with Reshaping Your Life?

Everything. If you are here, you are moving forward. But you need more than your head in the game. This is about your life, your mind, your personality, your values, your vision, your relationships, your health, and your body. You need it all to make progress.

The human body was built to move. But to stay safe, you have to be tuned up and turned on so you can reduce the effects of stress. Think about keeping your car tuned up. If you don't oil it, gas it, and do some basic preventive maintenance on it, one day it just won't go.

Human bodies work the same way. What keeps you in tune is walking, doing chores, playing games, dancing, stretching and the like. We humans have been hunting, gathering, running and relaxing for millions of years. Today's stresses, though, kick us into high gear for fear responses far more often than these bodies were built to tolerate. Ten thousand years ago cortisol and adrenaline — the hormones that get us revved up to move fast when something stresses us — were used primarily to run from beasts and bad weather. Today, the beasts come in the form of testy relationships — from bosses to siblings, and from parents to significant others. And the storms come from pressure to perform and to conform.

It's time to relieve your stress. Here you will find a variety of techniques to help you manage stress in your daily life.

Our bodies require movement to push the effects of stress out of our way. Movement gets the organs in our bodies to release toxins, and gets our cerebral-spinal fluid (the equivalent of oil for our brains and nervous systems) greasing our neurons, so our brains can fire up and do their job properly.

So movement has everything to do with shaping your life, making choices and finding the next opportunity in your life. A stagnant body produces a stagnant mind. And you are striving to be in the exact opposite place of stagnation right now — you're out for change, adventure, finding your place in the world. Moving into a new kind of work will take moving your state of mind as well as moving your state of body. So let's look more into the benefits of movement.

The Psychological and Intellectual Benefits of Movement

Have you heard the expression, "Take a walk to clear your head"? We humans intuitively know that the best way to clear our minds is to move our bodies. Why is that? It's because movement actually affects how the brain works. Physical activity — the movement of muscles — stirs up the release of neurotrophins. These are handy things that stimulate nerve growth and improve our neural network. Add to that all the things we've read in the popular press about endorphins and other "feel good" hormones that are released when we exercise — and why would we want to live without this?

Let's talk about the neural network for a minute. Just like the strength of your outside network — connections which move you to the next opportunity — your inside network is powerful beyond belief. By feeding your neural network through physical movement and intention, you build strong links that allow you to make connections faster, see things more clearly, and change more quickly. Carla Hannaford, in *Smart Moves,* calls the neural network the superhighway to development. The more on and off ramps you build, the more capabilities you can access and the quicker you can get there.

So it's pretty hard to argue against movement. With an expanded neural network, cerebral-spinal fluid greasing the wheels of the network, and muscle movement growing your nerves, you can do anything you set your mind to.

What If You Don't Exercise or Move Now?

If you're conscious, you are moving. Maybe you're not moving enough to optimize that brain of yours for change, but just moving is a great start. Really feeling good, in high gear, and ready for anything does require vibrant movement. This doesn't mean you have to run a marathon or train for a football team, but it does mean paying attention to your body, how it feels, and how it works for you or against you.

While I'm not going to instruct you on all the dos and don'ts of physical fitness, I do want you to know how to use your body to get your mind to work better for you. We are built as a dynamic, integrated system — our mind affects our body and vice versa. When your body is strong, so is your mind. There are more neural pathways available to you, and more ways to relieve stress, increase your mental sharpness and have the endurance for marathon thinking and brainstorming sessions.

PAY ATTENTION
Your body
What's your next move?

The first step is to move more often. For example, don't let yourself sit at your computer for more than fifty minutes at a time without getting up and stretching and walking around. Every twenty to thirty minutes is even better.

The second step is to walk more, whether it's around the house or the yard or up the stairs in your apartment building. Walking clears the head because you get into a rhythm, you swing your arms, and you get both sides of your body and your brain working at the same time. This shakes out the cobwebs. If you're not a regular exerciser, then start with short fifteen- to twenty-minute walks (preferably outside — but a treadmill or around the house is OK too). If you can walk every day, great — if not, start with three times a week. And of course, be mindful of your overall health, and ask a doctor if you are ready to begin a regular exercise routine.

The third step is to begin choosing fun ways to add movement to your life. Anything goes here! Dance, jump around, throw a stick for your dog, skate, bicycle, play pickup basketball or anything else that pleases you. I do a little bit of jogging several times a week. I have to admit, I don't love to jog, but I do love the way I feel when I'm done. And I like the pride I have in running, since it came to me as a sport later in life. So when I add it all up, it pleases me a great deal to run. The number one thing about this is that it's fun — otherwise you won't keep doing it.

Lastly, move every day, in some way. Some days it may be a six-mile walk, and some days it may be doing the laundry or raking leaves (my Zen side remembers that these can be enjoyed as well, if I choose to enjoy them!). If you care enough about your health to brush your teeth every day, then you can care enough to move every day for both mental and physical well-being.

Movement Choices

I have three separate sections below for movement activities. First, I talk about ways to take short movement breaks while you're working at a desk or computer. Second, I talk about what we've learned from neuroscience and kinesiology, which is specifically designed to reduce stress and wake up your brain. Third, I talk about ideas on how to get moving and stay moving. All of these have references to online sources so you can see them in action.

Movement Breaks. Sitting too long makes you stiff and cranky. If you want to show yourself just how crunched up you get when you haven't been moving enough, try this out:

- Hold your arm in front of you, with your thumb up. With your eye on your thumb, guide your arm out to the side until it starts to feel uncomfortable. Repeat on the other side.
- Now do some gentle circles with your neck, a few times in one direction, then switch and repeat on the other side.
- Then grab your shoulder muscle between your neck and shoulder blade, squeeze gently and turn towards the shoulder you are massaging. Repeat on the other side. Breathe.
- Finally, put one arm and thumb out, again tracking your thumb and see how far you can go. I'll bet it's a lot looser and you have turned farther.

This only takes a couple of minutes and gives you a great sense of how important a little movement is to keeping your brain and body flexible. It shows you right away how movement can release stress.

It's amazing, isn't it, what a difference a little movement can make? Get out of that chair now and try one or more of the following:

- Dance to favorite music
- Stretch — arms overhead, touch your toes (keep your knees slightly bent so you don't stress your back), swing from side to side
- Skip around the house
- Jump, even do jumping jacks

- Walk around the house
- Do a chore that gets you bending and twisting, like laundry, loading the dishwasher, mopping the floor
- At least tilt from side to side in your chair, circle your hips, and twist back and forth to release tension

If you're like me and sometimes your brain goes dead on ideas to get moving, try going online and doing some activities like stretching and yoga at your desk. Here are a couple of links that I like, but I'm sure you can find more, as new stuff is out there all the time. Type in "desk stretch" or "desk workout," "yoga at your desk," "yoga at your computer" or "desk exercise" when you do the search and you should find some good ideas.

Here are a couple that I really like:

1. From the U.S. government check out www.smallstep.gov. It gives a great overview of health and physical activity.

2. This one is from the Province of Alberta in Canada, and they really did their homework. You can reach them at www.centre4activeliving.ca/workplace.

They have two series: one on stretching at your desk, and the other on yoga at your desk. Both are great, and a little different from each other.

Lessons from Neuroscience and Kinesiology. About ten years ago I was co-facilitating a workshop for about 300 corporate executives. The facilitation team was not getting along too well. One of our members suggested we use a movement and joint goal setting technique together to de-stress and get back on our game. So we agreed to do a series of physical movements designed to do just that. I didn't believe such a simple process could make a difference, but it did. The team leader chilled out, people stopped yelling, and we managed to put our best foot forward for the rest of the conference.

I got hooked. I wanted to know more. So I started taking classes, and ended up getting licensed to teach and consult using educational kinesiology techniques. It's a way to connect physical movement with a mental workout to reduce stress and increase focus. I have used it in large corporate training groups and in coaching people one-on-one. I use it every time I work with groups, especially large ones where I need all my energy available to respond to all the different needs. It is one of the best ways I know to get yourself hooked up and ready to learn and take on new challenges.

Mind-body processes like these ask you to set a goal, engage in movement, then restate or refocus your goal when you're done. It is a balancing process. You may do it already just by announcing you need to take a walk or a run to clear your head.

The only thing is, we often don't give ourselves a moment when we're done to refocus ourselves, to set our own restart button. So look at the steps below, and start thinking about closing the circuit as you clear your head and reset yourself.

1. Set focus or goal —

Talk to yourself about the issue you want to resolve, then state it as a goal rather than a complaint.

2. Move —

Feel the issue in your body —get clear on where the stress is. Send your breath there to release it.

3. Reset —

Take a moment to identify what's changed for you after your walk, run, etc.— and what can be different now.

Here's an example:

1. Set — I'm getting hyper about finishing this project today and I'm starting to make mistakes. I need a walk. My goal is to calm down so the ideas can percolate to the surface.

2. Move — I start the walk and my hips feel really stiff, my knees are achy. Don't forget to breathe and let the walk just take over for me.

3. Reset — I've blown off some steam, I can sit down at my computer now and concentrate. I'll focus on letting the work flow, rather than pushing so hard.

Whether it's yoga, tai chi or a mind-body workout spawned by the latest research in neuroscience, it's really a flow of activities designed to loosen you up so you can accomplish your goals more effectively. I don't see it as any different from a series of warm-up activities that get you ready to play a sport or dance a ballet. The difference is that moving with intention to re-set your nervous system is simply warming up your body to allow your brain to perform at peak levels. We feel "on" when it all works together and our energy is flowing.

Get Moving and Stay Moving. As I said above, you can do just about anything — as long as it moves your body. If you're starting to feel motivated to find a regular exercise routine, this is where you can find some ideas to motivate you.

I found a great site online with just about every idea I could think of to do fun stuff to get you moving. What I love about this site is that it's actually focused on kids (www.bam.gov). But don't let that scare you away. It's focused on having fun, so it taps into the kid in all of us. Best of all, it has a broad list of ideas for activity.

It might help take you back to when you were a kid and reconsider doing something you loved to do then. For example, were you a big skater? If that's what you love — don't force yourself into jogging just because it's the adult thing to do. DO WHAT YOU LOVE! Then you can love what you do — it applies to getting and staying active as much as it does to finding work you love.

If you can't get online, here's a quick list of easy activities anyone can do. Don't forget to consult www.smallstep.gov and www.bam.gov when you have a minute.

Quick Tips for Easy Activities

- Walk, cycle, jog, skate, etc., around the neighborhood or to work, school, the store
- Park the car farther away from your destination
- Get on or off the bus or metro a stop earlier
- Take the stairs instead of the elevator or escalator
- Join a volleyball (lacrosse, basketball, etc.) league
- Take dance lessons
- Play with children or pets — everybody wins
- Take fitness breaks — walking or doing desk exercises — instead of taking cigarette or coffee/soda breaks
- Take care of your house yourself — gardening or home repair activities
- Do yoga, tai chi, martial arts
- Take classes at your local Y or activity center
- Use leg power — take small trips on foot to get your body moving
- Dance to music or just jump around for no reason
- Keep a pair of comfortable running shoes in your car and office — be ready for activity wherever you go
- Take movement breaks often while working

Strategy: Move More to Create More

1. What simple, five minute tactic can you add to your daily computer or desk time to get you up and moving? For example, I throw the ball with my dog every so often to shake out the cobwebs.

   Your tactic: _____

2. What new activity can you add to your schedule on a weekly basis to move and get creative in a different way? For example, my husband and I started ballroom dancing classes (that will work your left brain and your right brain — follow the steps, and flow with the music).

   Your tactic: _____

Your brain relies on your body's energy to do its work — your brain can take you where you've never gone before only if your body is able to transport it there. So go, move — it opens doors for engaging the world.

WHAT-WHERE-WHO-Now?

What You'll Find

WHAT Now?

So you've done all this work and you think you've missed the mark. First, let's get clear on what the mark is not. It is not singularly about:

- Making a lot of money
- Gaining recognition and prestige

- Being blissfully happy every moment of your life
- Discovering the Job that makes you happy every minute of every day
- Never having to be concerned again about seeking your calling

Even though I've said it in the book, this is a process — like climbing a mountain, there's always another peak to bag. Our calling as human beings is to continue searching for what draws out the best in us. You will get some or all of the things on that list above throughout your life, just not every minute of every day.

Now let's get clear on what the mark IS:

- Leaving the past behind while acknowledging it is part of you
- Doing what satisfies you, energizes you, inspires you and contributes to the world
- Using your skills and talents, passions and abilities
- Focusing on right now

Your struggle likely comes from one of two places:

— You don't know what inspires you, and maybe even have never felt anything that really sparks you. This includes those of you who have been doing what someone else thinks you should do all your life.

— So many things excite you, you don't know which to choose. This includes those of you who have a bevy of talents to choose from and think you can do everything.

As I see it, you have two choices. You can either:

- Take whatever path presents itself now, and pay a lot of attention and ask a lot of questions, including understanding yourself better. Or,

- Keep trying lots of different things out, searching for a good focus to start with, and understanding yourself better.

The first path may be taking a job that is offered, even if you're not sure this is your direction. In uncertainty, take a leap and trust that you will learn something that will help you begin to narrow down the options and focus on your "sweet spot."

The second path may mean working temp jobs, volunteering, getting yourself involved in many different things to see more clearly what drives you. My friend Matt did just this. He found himself at times working two part-time jobs and volunteering. Wow! To me, that's impressive. It's so much more active and engaged in the world than just getting by. He was putting his feelers out and in that way, *figuring it out!*

Whichever path you choose, it looks like you need to dig a little deeper on understanding yourself and letting that guide your choices. You may need to step way out of your comfort zone to find what ignites you. Or you may need to concentrate your energy so you're not bouncing off the walls.

I don't want you to underestimate the learning curve on change — even at this stage you may still be easing into your target, or you're still learning how to handle the 3Fs — our fear responses of Flight, Fight, or Freeze. I don't have any magic wand answers. But you can pay closer attention to what's going on for you. When does your gut talk to you most strongly by flipping and flopping? What turns you on the most about the things you are currently working on? What do your instincts tell you? Are you just floating? Are you trying too hard? Remember, your heart is faster than your head in figuring things out. Listen harder by giving yourself time to reflect, walk, journal, meditate, or get more coaching. Breathe, slow down.

PAY ATTENTION
Gut instinct

What's your next move?

If you need more help connecting your head to your heart, and your heart to your body, consider activities especially designed for that — from time honored practices like tai chi, qigong, yoga, and other martial arts, to newer programs based on the evolving field of neuroscience, that help the mind and the body to work together. Check out Section 4, *Movement,* for more ideas.

There is at least one clear clue to the difference between bobbing and weaving and needing a new WHAT: even as you bob and weave, you may find yourself coming back and pining after your declared WHAT, or some

PAY ATTENTION

Prevention

**What's your
next move?**

variation of it. If so, your WHAT is still in the running. If not, you may need a different approach.

After having talked with your mentor and others about your WHAT, you may feel reticent about going back and telling them you need to rework your WHAT. Don't worry. In fact, this is a time to feel grateful that you are not cornering yourself into a future that isn't right for you. You're ahead of the game because you're paying better attention! Better now, than waking up in twenty years and finding out you have been working on someone else's WHAT.

This kind of thing can happen to any of us. We get lured, attracted, pushed, compromised into somebody else's WHAT. It's quite normal to be seduced into something attractive, familiar, or easy to reach. The great part is, you're paying attention right now, and you're looking at the WHAT and saying "Hmm, maybe I'm doing this because Dad wants me to, or because it's good money, or it looks stable and secure." But you know in your heart that you will find greater satisfaction elsewhere. Follow your heart — it will not steer you wrong. But heart alone won't get you to your goal. You will need to reinvest in the *Discovery* process to get on the right track.

So you end up deciding that you've got the wrong WHAT — Big deal. Circle back and reexamine your WHAT. You may also want to get a little better acquainted with yourself. I suggest you consider taking some profiles of your thinking style and your values. My favorite profiles can be found later in this section and I can help you set them up.

By the way, if you need a little confidence building, even if you are reinforced on the WHAT you are following — do these instruments. They'll help you feel surer of yourself because they enhance your understanding of why you're choosing your WHAT-WHERE-WHO. This can make you feel good about your choice, and gives you personal insights that will contribute to successful interviews and job choices.

If you need to circle back and start again, you may find your mentor had a few doubts of her own. Despite this, she may well have felt you needed to explore the first avenue to be sure. Good coaches know there is a readiness factor. There's an old Chinese proverb that says, "When the student is ready, the teacher will appear."

You probably weren't ready in the first round to see what you see now. When you're fighting yourself (Fight), or running away from commitment (Flight) or standing still and doing nothing (Freeze), no one can jostle you out of where you are just by talking to you. You needed to travel this far up the mountain to get to a point where you could see the whole panorama of *you* more clearly. Your mentor will be a great help as you rediscover the better path — she, too, knows more about you to help you now.

How to Circle Back

If you're totally in the wrong WHAT, start over. Reread your past timeline to start figuring out what other possibilities are out there. You may not yet know what it is, but you know what it's not. Good step. Don't underestimate knowing your mismatch; you've gotten a lot further than many who never look. Revitalize your timeline if you need to, and do some more research — on yourself and on opportunities. Turn on the seasoned performer interviews again. The next strategy walks you through a series of questions to help you determine what parts of your plan you may want to reshape.

⚙ *Strategy: Circling Back Questions*

Determine the focus of your circle back activities and whether you need to consider hiring a coach.

1. **Ask yourself the 3Ws again.** What do you want to be now? Where do you want to be? Who do you want to be with? Determine your least understood questions and where you need to do the most work.

2. **What is the next move you need to make?** Do you need to start over? Do you need to repeat some of the activities? Do you need to redraft your plan?

3. What question or issue might you be avoiding?

4. How can you keep this process simple, achievable, and less complicated? How can mentors or other supporters help? (Check the SMART questions again on page 111.)

5. How are you feeling as you begin the circle back process?

Note: It may help a lot to hire a professional coach at this point. I use them all the time in my work, especially when I know I'm stuck or just too close to the issue to see anything objectively. For more help on this, go to www. ChooseOnPurpose.com.

Think of this as a plateau on the mountain climb. You got a little lost, and now you are taking a breather, reorienting yourself, and getting back on track.

If you start trying lots of things out, be open to everything you are learning. Check yourself out against the first list above of what your mark is not, and stay focused on you (not your parents, family, friends, social expectations, etc.). I know it's easier said than done, but it's your life, after all. What do you want to do with it?

What if you don't know what it feels like to be passionate about something? Maybe you've never felt that chill up your spine, that feeling of pride for a job well done, a swell of energy to accomplish something so strong that you were willing to sacrifice other things to make it happen.

If so, then the best answer I have for you, besides trying things out, is to find someone who is passionate about what they do. It can range from a Y counselor who loves working with kids, to a pizza maker who prides herself on the best pizza in town. Hang out with those people, find out what drives them, what it feels like to have that zing of passion. They become your stand-ins, your "surrogates" for the experience. The power of that feeling can rub off on you, if you let it. So let's dive deeper into understanding yourself.

Understanding Yourself Better

There are lots of reasons why some people have an easier time at this than others. They range from personality to thinking style, and from upbringing to culture. Some of us have busy minds, others quiet minds. The busier our minds, the more challenging it can be to settle down and focus on ourselves.

There are three ways to understand yourself better:

- Ask other people for feedback
- Use reliable instruments to gain objective feedback
- Hire someone to help you

Each of these steps is simple, but not necessarily easy to do. They require patience, time and energy. And the second and third steps require some financial investment. Let's look at each of these separately.

Ask others for feedback. Sometimes it's as simple as asking for help. Approach three people who know you well and ask them to think about the following questions and then meet with you to debrief the answers:

Strategy: Get Feedback

Understand your strengths, limitations and potential contribution.

1. **Strengths.** What three adjectives describe your personal strengths? Of those, which one is your outstanding, best descriptor? (See Descriptor List below for help with adjectives.)

2. **Limitations.** Understanding that your strengths in excess become your limitations, which adjective, when you do it in excess, do you need to be most aware of managing? For example, you may be very spontaneous, but in excess this can feel chaotic, disorganized, or like lack of planning.

3. **Contribution.** Ask your friends to identify the top three things you contribute. This can help answer what kinds of things you contribute to any kind of work you do, whether hobby, associating with friends, or job. The kinds of things they might answer include: an eye for detail, creative ideas, creating a plan, getting things done, taking care of people's feelings.

Based on input from others, complete the sentence:

We can count on you to contribute_____.

Debrief this input with friends and mentor then match it up with help from Section 1: *Picture Work You Love.* Or, continue below with additional kinds of help.

Descriptor List

Adaptable	*Dogmatic*	*Opinionated*
Analytical	*Easygoing*	*Organized*
Appreciative	*Encouraging*	*Patient*
Blunt	*Energetic*	*Pressuring*
Compromising	*Fair*	*Reflective*
Conservative	*Forceful*	*Reserved*
Considerate	*Guarded*	*Resourceful*
Critical	*Impatient*	*Self-centered*
Decisive	*Impulsive*	*Self-confident*
Delegating	*Independent*	*Self-controlled*
Demanding	*Initiating*	*Supportive*
Dependable	*Methodical*	*Trustworthy*
Detached	*Moody*	*Understanding*
Determined	*Open-minded*	

Use Reliable Instruments. There are more self-assessment instruments out there than boulders on a mountain path. So rather than confuse you with dancing around trying out any number of them (I've done enough of this for the both of us!), I'm going to point you towards two approaches. You may want to use one or both, but they do different things.

The first approach focuses on understanding your thinking style and values. It includes two online instruments, the first called the Herrmann Brain Dominance Instrument (HBDI), and the second, called My Motivators. They target understanding values and thinking preferences and how that can affect life and career choices.

The second approach focuses on understanding your aptitudes and competencies — what you're good at. It aims to help you understand your skills, abilities, and interests.

Each approach — detailed below — requires a financial investment on your part. They are proven and reliable ways to deepen your self-knowledge and I highly recommend them.

Approach 1: Thinking style and values. Your thinking style helps determine what you are interested in, and ultimately the kinds of things you might be motivated to do. The more you know about your preferences, the easier it is to work in your "sweet spot." It's just like knowing you have a preference for right- or left-handedness. Sure, you can use the other hand, but it will be a lot more effort. I use the HBDI for this.

The second aspect of self-understanding is getting clear on your values — what drives you to be happy and satisfied with your life. The more you get what motivates you to act and achieve in this world, the more likely you are to create a good match for yourself. I use the My Motivators profile for this.

You can take one or both of these instruments, and you can even combine the results of the two to understand your motivators more thoroughly. By combining the results you will be better able to see how your values and your thinking style interact.

Some of us have more complex interactions than others, and our values can conflict with our thinking preferences. For example, I love to coach and work on a team, and have a high value for humanitarian efforts. But I also like to control and influence the outcomes of projects I'm involved in. So this need to influence can get in the way of the need to be collaborative in a team effort. I have to determine what kinds of results I want, and how to balance these often-conflicting waves inside of me.

Some of us have multiple drivers, which can conflict with each other, and may confuse us in getting clear on our strengths and motivators. These instruments could help some of you who have a more complex mix of motivators and preferences sort through your abilities and interests.

Check out the Web site at www.ChooseOnPurpose.com for details on purchasing these instruments and hiring some coaching assistance.

Approach 2: Aptitudes and competencies. Some of us can benefit from examining our abilities with more scrutiny. The well-reputed Johnson O'Connor Foundation has been researching and assisting people to identify their skills and abilities for over half a century. In order to take their assessments, you will need to visit them in a major city and take hands-on tests to determine very concretely your abilities and interests. Their work includes personal coaching and feedback, and is well worth the investment for those who need more tangible information. You will find them on the Web at www.jocrf.org.

Hire Someone to Help You. Sometimes we just need a little outside, objective help. Our own opinion and that of our friends may be a little too close to be impartial. I've had many great coaches over my lifetime, and they've made a huge difference. Most recently, my husband and I took up ballroom dancing. Wow — you want to talk about a place where you need neutral feedback! Like the change you are going through now, there is intricate footwork, timing, rhythm and concentration required. We couldn't do it without a teacher who simply calls us on our mistakes, without the bias and emotion each of us would have laid on each other. Coaching works!

Investigate the coaching options at www.ChooseOnPurpose.com. We have many excellent coaches, and there are many others out there, should you choose a different route. Your needs are unique, so look for someone that will click with you, but also challenge you. I have a bias for giving you the scoop directly, so our coaching uses the straight-shooter approach. We want to get to the core quickly and give you practical steps to take.

One more thing. Please don't think there's something wrong with you if you decide to get some coaching. Corporate executives pay thousands of dollars to talk to someone who is objective and gets to the point without having to be politically smooth. Everyone needs coaching. Whether it's a tip from a loved one on how to handle a situation, or guidance on major decisions — our biases need some balancing

The bottom line — coaches can help pull you out of the mud. They give you a checkpoint, a schedule, and something to do when you're struggling to figure it out. Don't be afraid to use them — it's all part of asking good questions to keep you moving forward.

Finally Hitting the Mark on Your WHAT. If you've been working the steps in this book, you may want to revisit some items, once you've got the additional insights from getting feedback, doing profiles, or using a coach. Whether you decide to take whatever is in front of you, or to keep actively trying new things out, you have more resources now to hit your mark.

Do the *Coffee House Blueprint* again — it has probably changed. This could tip you off to a new approach to your search, your questions, and your choices. Remember, it isn't a straight path, and part of it will always be in the dark forest, at least for a little while. But these steps keep you from retracing your first path over and over again.

WHERE Now?

A Bug for Adventure. As I was completing this book, two young friends of mine, Joe and Rachael, had just finished a two-month cross-country tour. They had saved up a couple thousand bucks each, and set out by car, stopping at friends along the way. They saw the country, tasted food in the South and the West, and camped out on the beaches of Hawaii.

Rachael wanted to move from Philadelphia to San Francisco, and stayed behind, starting a brand-new life by waiting tables her first couple of months to get settled and get started. Joe, who had commitments to a family business, drove back home, but a changed man. The time and the space helped him see what he really wanted to do. He will complete his commitments within the year, then travel to Australia and New Zealand, like he has always wanted to, then move to the West Coast, to work in the vineyards.

Rachael and Joe are classic examples of getting up and getting moving — creating space to discover what's next. They embraced adventure and moved towards it. The result was life-changing and uplifting. Some of us really do need a change of place to stir up our creative juices.

If you need a change of WHERE, it is as simple as moving. You put yourself first. It's not selfish — in fact, it's very giving. How else can you figure out what you're here to do? By taking care of yourself, you will be able to take care of others and your piece of the world.

Just do it. No one can help you in such a decision or do it for you. If you want it, you will find a way to make it happen. Joe and Rachael did. You can too.

Considering the Elements of Your Personal WHERE. If you see yourself living in a particular region that offers something that you will enjoy, what is stopping you from going there? If it is the draw of family, or stability, then recognize that you are making a deliberate choice of having that over the different environment. The key here is deliberate choice — and once you make it, to make peace with it.

Strategy: Investigate WHERE

How does WHERE affect you? What kind of place (mental or physical) brings out the best in you?

1. **Answer these questions first:**
   - Where do you dream about living?
   - What would that environment offer you?
   - What kind of community would you like to be in?
   - What would make you happy about that place?
   - Who would be there that would complement you?
   - What could you do there — work, play, people that would satisfy you and make you feel complete?
   - How much of your WHERE can be created by your own state of mind? By creating your own community — your own sense of place — right where you are?

2. **Then answer these questions:**
   - What keeps you planted where you are?
   - What do you like most about it?
   - What do you like least?
   - How does your WHERE line up with your values and interests?
   - Where would you NOT want to live? Why?
   - Could you live anywhere? Why or why not?

3. **Do your homework.** Matching yourself to the world is about place as much as people and work.

4. **Work towards a choice,** now that you have a better idea of what you're looking for:

Draw a T-chart on a piece of paper (a line down the middle of your page, with a column header for each side — in this case "Why stay" and "Why go." Let the weight of the arguments on each side, not just the number of items, steer you in the direction of making a choice. Then make the decision, own it, and make the decision right.

WHO Now?

It may be stating the obvious — but where you live and what you want to do dramatically affect who shows up in your life. If you wait tables in a beach town in California, you will spend a lot of time with tourists, vacationers, and people soaking up the sun. If you work in a research lab, you will end up spending time with people busy solving problems, figuring out answers to complex questions, and seeking to make new discoveries in the world. Your location determines who shows up in your life.

This is not a book about personal relationships and how to manage them. But I wouldn't be doing my job if I didn't include a short mention of what you want to do about the people in your life. Place makes a difference, as does your attitude and the people you draw towards you. While you can't control the actions of others, much of the time you attract the people in your life that you want to be around. You choose who stays and who goes. Your behavior pulls or pushes.

Sometimes toxic people show up, and you need to keep your distance. You can choose to send them on their way. When you do, it is with respect and good wishes. It isn't always easy, or quick, but it can be done. I've done it twice in my life, and while it was emotional, it was necessary for me to stay healthy and balanced. Creating a separation like this has fallout. I certainly felt it for weeks and months after. But I also felt relief — and the freedom to focus on myself.

Just like your work in this world, you want to run towards people you want to be around — seek out those who care. Surround yourself with the kinds of people you want in your life. Where you choose to live and what you choose to do determines who you will be around.

I choose to do yoga, so I end up hanging out with people who love to stay fit and are dedicated to a regular practice. This is motivating. I love being married — so I volunteer to work with young couples preparing for marriage, and to work with a team of married couples who feel the same way I do about marriage. I love small town life and community work, so I spend many hours working on community improvement projects with interesting, challenging, and dedicated people who inspire me every day. What I do and where I live absolutely determine who I spend my time with.

The more you know about your values and what you love spending your time on, the easier it becomes to target the kinds of people you want to be around. It ranges from a lacrosse team, to co-workers, to volunteering in an animal shelter and beyond. The possibilities are endless — because people's passions and interests are boundless. Here is a way to think about who you want to surround yourself with.

Strategy: Investigate WHO

Identify the elements of who you want in your life.

1. Answer these questions:

- Where do you want to spend your time?

- Who is there?

- Are these the kinds of people you want to be around? Why? Why not?

- Where else could you spend your time to attract the kinds of people you want in your life?

- What kinds of groups or communities attract the kinds of people you want to spend time with?

2. Complete this sentence:

The attributes of people I want to spend my time with include

_____.

Once you have answers to these questions, you are well on your way to shaping the WHERE and WHO Now in your life. And like all the choices we talk about here — choose them on purpose.

Managing Parents
and Family

What You'll Find

Defining Parent Management

Before we begin talking about this subject, let's explore what I mean by managing your parents (and other key people who influence your life, like brothers and sisters, extended family and mentors). Some people get a strong reaction to the very idea of managing. Especially your parents. It sounds contrary to normal thinking about family relationships, and maybe even a little bigheaded. Why the word managing?

Let's look at some definitions of manage: be in charge of; administer and regulate; succeed in doing, achieving, or producing something especially difficult. I particularly like the last part of the definition. Let's concentrate on producing something that can be difficult to accomplish during a transition like this — a great, supportive, and liberating relationship with your parents.

The challenge comes in the very idea of managing your parents at all — especially as a twentysomething. You've been doing it, though, for quite a long time. It probably included sweet talking Dad into shopping money when you were a teenager, or convincing Mom to let you hang out in town unsupervised with your friends. Now we're talking about evolving a relationship to its next level — and you taking your share of the responsibility for making it work. And I think that's why we don't talk about it much. It requires energy and courage to set new expectations.

The Nature of This Transition

As a parent myself, I admit that it rankles me to think about being managed by my kids. Why? I think mostly because I spent a lot of years managing *them*. It's just plain hard to think about the tables being turned. As a parent, at one point of my kids' lives, I managed every detail — from what they ate to where they went and who they played with. Then, before we know it, this supervisor role is shifting to advisor role. And the typical reaction of most parents, including me, goes something like . . . "So, what's this, then?!"

A great example of this shake-up occurred as my kids' friends entered their twenties. I have always asked them at this point to start calling me Susan. This took some adjustment for me, but going from Mrs. Berg to Susan is way harder for them.

The calling out of a name is a clear marker that something has changed — and we trip over it for a while. The discomfort of breaking an old habit shows itself loud and clear, first in disbelief that it's OK to call me Susan, then later, when they get that worried look that maybe they're not being respectful. And sometimes I contribute to it, with a puzzled look, not remembering for a moment that things are changing.

Unfortunately, most of us don't stop calling our parents by the name we grew up with — Mom continues to be Mom, and Dad, Dad. So there's no clear rite of passage towards peer relationships with parents. It's not a faucet you can just turn off one day, but more like a river cutting a new course. And the same kinds of feelings are going on — worry, second-guessing — it's just that most of them are flowing underground. And of course, relationships with parents are more complicated. You never lose that unique parent-child bond. But evolve it must, if all of us are to move successfully on to the next stage of our lives.

So, while as a parent it might not excite me to know I'm becoming your peer, and indeed being managed, I am very well aware that it is happening. And not only is that OK, it's healthy and the way it should be, especially when we define managing as achieving something that is particularly challenging.

But not all parents see it this way — and neither do I sometimes (in my weaker moments). We begin to feel less able to influence your decisions anymore. This makes us a little sensitive, and we need to be handled with care. That's where managing comes in — finding the balance between us wanting things to be the way they used to be — and you wanting to pave your own way.

PAY ATTENTION
Handle with care

What's your
next move?

So as a parent myself, I'm going to take the plunge on behalf of my children and other parents and advise you — go ahead and manage me! I'm not saying we parents are going to love this at first, or maybe even ever, but it's part of you becoming grown up, and part of us accepting the next stage of

life. If you do this actively, with intention, you'll have a lot more success at it than if you give in to the urge to roll your eyes, pout, or get mad.

Why Manage Your Parents

Why should you manage your parents, and what benefits will you get from it?

You may be able to:

- Lessen their worrying about you and release some tension in the house and the relationship.
- Help them relax so you won't feel as much pressure from them.
- Learn to rely on your parents as consultants, rather than supervisors or even best buddies, so you can make your own decisions and your own mistakes.
- Make them feel good about their parenting skills, so you will get help when you ask for it and freedom when you need it.
- Build your adult child-parent bond, so you can have a happier life.

When you look at it this way, positively managing your parents becomes a no-brainer — because you see all the productive paybacks. So let's look at the kinds of challenges that often come with this kind of transition.

How to Manage Your Parents. Change isn't a straight path. You will circle the same territory, make some jumps, and tread water at times. Here are three common challenges you'll deal with.

Challenge 1: Push back and back-tracking. Twenty years of habits are hard to break. As parents, we will still want to control your life at times — mostly because we want to protect you. Be patient with us and expect us to try to turn the clock back from time to time.

Give us a wide berth and the space to respond positively. It really doesn't help when you give us even the slightest excuse to get defensive, or God forbid, start with the "I changed your diapers and fed you since you were a baby, etc., . . ." story. The last thing you want at a time like this is what, in our family, we call a "stack attack." These are the arguments where we all start digging into our baggage to inform each other, yet again, of all the grievances we have from situations and disagreements long past. No. This digs us all in deeper.

Instead, step out and manage us during these times by reassuring us and keeping your cool. Try not to get angry or overbearing yourself. And look for the balance between asking for support versus leaning on us too much. Sometimes you unwittingly ask to be treated like a kid and want someone else to make the decisions for you.

This is part of that back-tracking thing. It's common when things are changing to want to go back to what we're comfortable with. Some of this is normal. But it also gets confusing — parents hear, "Let me go!" one minute, then, "Take care of me!" the next. While it's bound to happen, just notice it and point it out. Then you have something to talk about and even laugh about. And remember, we parents and kids really are doing the best we can.

Challenge 2: Emotions running high. The best you can do in your relationship is to be honest, open, respectful and considerate. You cannot control your parents and how they feel, and in fact, you (and your parents) will struggle with controlling much of anything at times, except maybe the expression of your emotions. Often, we can't even control our own emotions in changeovers like this, as they sweep over us when we least expect it. But we might be able to control how we express them.

For example, when we're angry, we have the split second choice of saying something mean, or asking for a moment to collect our thoughts. Good critical choices are made when we focus on the smallest step that is right in front of us. So rejecting your parents' opinions outright may make you feel like you are in control, but it's nothing more than a momentary perception. And the opposite is true too — taking what they say as gospel and not taking your own stand results in a feeling of no control, which hurts just as much.

So when emotions run high, try these responses:

Tips for Handling Emotional Conversations

Help steer the conversation with questions and statements like:

- Let's step back a minute
- What are we trying to accomplish here?
- Let's take a breather

Mellow out your tone of voice

- Soften up the prickliness of your raw emotions
- Maybe even get parents to open up a bit about what they're afraid of on your behalf
- Use the attitude in your voice to get us really talking, so good things can happen

Prepare your parents to listen instead of attempting to control how they will react. Ask things like:

- What are you thinking about? Why?
- What do you need from me right now?
- How do you want this to turn out?

Surprises always happen in human relationships, but the more you focus on facilitating — opening the channels and greasing the skids, and the less you worry about controlling your parents — the more likely you'll get closer to what you need.

Challenge 3: The "I told you so" speech. It's bound to happen. We parents want so much to spare you the pain of learning things for yourself, that we overdo the supervising and empathy behaviors at times like this. Your parents will see you do things they know you will regret. But you're going to have to do some of these things anyway, and trip over your own feet. We parents have short memories about the things we had to do for ourselves. And sometimes things will work in your favor, and sometimes they won't.

The best way to handle the times when they don't is to mature into some humility. When the "I told you so" moment comes at our house, we often don't even have to say the words "I told you so"; the look between us says it all. While it may sting a little at first, try to swallow it gracefully, go with the flow and move past it.

In our family, we have learned to laugh together at this stuff. Erik, my son, who is so light-hearted and able to live in the moment, will roll his eyes (in humor) at us, laugh and say, "I know, you don't even have to say it, I screwed this up!" And Kirstin, our daughter, who has a more tempered and serious approach, will hold a discussion with us on what she has learned from the experience.

But this took time to develop. Don't forget that practice makes progress, in all things, especially relationship management. And of course, the situation has flipped, since they know us well too. We have had to swallow the humble pie more than once and let them bask in an "I told you so!" moment.

Tips for Managing Your Parents in Times of Flux

While there are countless tips that can help as you shift this relationship, here are four that I believe helped my family and our friends.

- Set expectations together
- Listen first, then talk
- Be consistent, seek balance
- Encourage parents to let go

Here are some details about each of these.

- **Set expectations together.** We've talked in the book about how important it is to set expectations for your own future. Now it's time to set expectations for your future with your parents and other loved ones. Your life is changing and the best way to handle differences is to call them out and establish ground rules for behavior. Key things to talk about include:

- **Family time together.**
  - What are your responsibilities to one another — from cooking dinner and holiday time, to handling disputes and making big decisions
  - Schedules — including work, play, time to yourself
  - Desires for WHERE you want to be — nearby or traveling afar — and how you will manage your family responsibilities

You'll talk about these in steps. Being aware of these key issues, and the particular needs of your family, is an important first step. When you don't state your expectations, confusion and disappointment can mushroom. Take the lead and start the conversation. The strategy below walks you through two sample conversations to get things started.

Strategy: Set Expectations Together

Hold purposeful conversations with your parents and family members about what is changing in your life.

1. Talk about the changes you are undergoing and what it feels like. The first step is to simply open the channel of communication. Find a comfortable time and location — after a family dinner, or maybe even out together for breakfast, where you don't have any distractions and everyone is fresh.

It might go like this: *"Mom and Dad, let's talk about what's going to happen over these next few months as I start to figure out my next moves. What do you see ahead of us? What's on your mind right now?"*

256

Listen for what's on their minds, then tell them how you're feeling. *"I'm feeling anxious to get some new things going. I want to really dig into this search, but I know I'm going to be a little moody at times, so I may need some extra space."*

2. As you progress in your search, you will discover more needs to set clear expectations and boundaries. Try to anticipate as best you can when it's time to take the next conversation step.

Something like this: *"Mom and Dad, let's talk about some of these information interviews I'm going on and how I'm spending my time. I want you to understand how I'm doing this and why I may not be able to do some things you used to expect of me."*

You may go on to explain that you will be away, that you won't be telling them every detail of every interview, or that you won't be taking that job they thought was perfect for you. Explain what you're doing, the time and responsibility boundaries you need, and why.

3. Identify an area that you need to talk to your parents about. Think about both their needs and feelings and your own. Get clear on the outcome you want. Then find a time to open the channel of communication and discuss mutual expectations.

Conversations like this encourage your parents to think with you instead of for you. When you start to get frustrated, try one of these questions. Better dialogue comes in baby steps. Let your parents know when you disagree and you're going to take an action that they find unsuitable for you. For your parents, knowing what to expect is a lot better than being left in the dark.

Sometimes the best thing you can do to encourage us to let you go is to be prudent and timely about when you tell us things. You may need to play your hand, and figure out where things are going before you tell us about it. Tempted though you may be to spill your guts, it may be better to find a friend who can serve as your foil while you let things unfold. A story that is progressing may be just the thing to encourage us to support you, despite our doubts and questions. Timing is everything.

257

- **Listen first, then talk.** Start listening more closely to what your parents need from you. Look to understand what is important for them to know, and where you can set boundaries. Don't hide important stuff, but don't feel you have to betray your own need for privacy and self-discovery either.

Some information is way better than none, from a parent's perspective. And the more you let us know what your own boundaries are, the more likely it is we will gradually learn to respect and live with those. But don't expect miracles overnight. Remember — we're coming off twenty years of managing you — so being managed by you is a big switch for us.

Both of my kids have learned how much better things go when we have at least some information about their lives. My son, Erik, is much more private, yet he has developed a keen ability to tell me a little about what's going on, and that way he has alleviated my need to pry and nudge (as much as I used to). Not that I still don't try. But we have grown a lot together in our relationship after he entered the army. Erik made a big jump (for us, anyway), and we weathered a few storms in developing our adult relationship to get to a good level of mutual respect for guarding boundaries, while at the same time feeling included.

The most memorable example of this transition period came during his first leave home after boot camp. It was Christmas time, and we barely saw him except for Christmas day. When he left, my husband, Jim, and I were both angry and hurt. While we realized he was going through a huge transition, SO WERE WE! In our eyes, we had just been pushed into a transition we thought would take a few years, in just a few months. We were a little shell-shocked.

But rather than harboring our anger, the two of us talked through what was happening to all of us. My husband and I realized that we had not made clear to Erik what our needs were, and that he probably didn't even know yet what he needed, he was so overwhelmed by the changes he was going through. And we also knew in our hearts that he was breaking away from us in a good way — and needed more space to accomplish that. So Jim and I decided to call Erik and explain how we felt. He listened, carefully, and really heard us. Then he took steps to actively manage the situation.

The upshot has been a much stronger effort at talking to each other before actions are taken. For example, Erik will now tell us what his anticipated schedule is before he comes home on leave, and ask when we would like him around for dinner or family activities. Yes indeed — he's doing a good job of managing us — and our expectations. The net result is a much more relaxed visit and much more meaningful conversation among all the family members.

And new, yet important, little practices have sprung up. In our case, it's how we communicate by telephone. It's always the little things that make a difference, like when I say good-bye on the phone, I almost always say, "Love you." He now says it back, and means it. For us, it is a sign of mutual respect and dedication to maintaining our family connection.

- **Be consistent, seek balance,** at least as much as you can. This one is hard — you want independence and support at the same time. It can get confusing when you push us away then reel us back in by calling us with every little detail of your life. It's oh so easy for parents to get sucked back into the details. The rub is, the more confusing it gets, the harder it is to set expectations of one another for leading our own lives and making our own decisions.

So take the time to understand your unique relationship with your parents. Keep your eye on the balance between independence and control, support and self-determination. The more you talk about your needs and listen to those of your parents, the more likely you can be consistent, because they will be able to remind you of the expectations you set together.

- **Encourage parents to let go.** You don't do this by saying these exact words to us, but by giving us reason to believe that you are working things out in your own way. Take action to make something new happen in your life, like what the *Discovery* process in the book charts out.

259

Actions speak louder than words, and as we watch you work at this, our faith in you, and our willingness to let go, grows stronger.

My daughter, Kirstin, is particularly good at this. She is not afraid to give us critical feedback when we need it — she lets us know outright when we have overstepped our boundaries. But she does it in a way that is not judgmental, but feels good for us. She has successfully turned the tables and learned how to coach her own parents. What this leads to is more open-ended conversation, and more opportunity for self-improvement for all of us.

This was particularly noteworthy a couple of years after she graduated from college. She was in the process of deciding to move from Washington, D.C. to Denver and stayed with us for six months during the transition period. Kirstin and my husband, Jim, and I all had a lot of time to talk about the decision she was making. We discussed cross-country moves, relationships, career and just about everything under the sun.

The beauty of this time period was our opportunity as parents to see her decision-making process up close. It increased our respect for her, and in the process, gave her more opportunity to create a strong adult relationship with us. And different from Erik, who needs his freedom from interference, Kirstin shares a lot and seeks a lot of input.

To keep things balanced, we have learned how important it is to create boundaries with her in the other directions — listening, but each side keeping enough objectivity and distance when it is needed. As a result, when she gives us feedback that she needs her space, or may be deciding on something we don't necessarily agree with, we still respect her for what she is doing and that she has kept us in the loop.

She has become very astute at asking open-ended questions of us. This includes things like, "What would you like to see me doing next in my life?" "What do you really think?"

I suggest you consider introducing these kinds of questions into your repertoire. They help you increase your listening time and give you more focused consulting time with your parents. Here are some questions that will encourage us parents to shift our conversations towards advising and away from supervising.

Conversation Starters with Your Parents
- What are you thinking about?
- What are you worried about?
- What would you do in my situation?
- What's different now from when you were my age that you see affecting my decisions?
- What suggestions do you have for next steps?
- What else could work here?
- What if we don't agree about what's next for me?
- What do you think I should pay attention to?
- What do you see that I don't?
- What do you think I see that you don't?
- How can we agree to disagree?

By setting expectations, listening and talking, trying to keep both yourself and your parents from being confused, you can help us to start letting go. Some parents have very precise ideas of what they expect of their kids. But don't make assumptions. Opening a real two-way conversation could be revealing, especially when you go into it with the agreement to explore and not to preach to each other. Nothing ventured, nothing gained. It's worth a try, and the results may be much better than you expect. You know the old saying, "Everything will be fine in the end." Just keep in mind that if it's not fine now, then it's simply not the end. Keep at it.

How to Chart Your Own Path

One of the hardest things to do is to strike out on a path — a productive and positive choice, not a harmful one — that is not the one your parents or family expected. But if that's what you need to do, then do it with confidence, faith in yourself, and belief in the support of your parents — if not now, then someday. Your choice may be foreign to your parents — persist anyway. Your choice may be contrary to your parents — persist anyway.

But how do you persist when they present an obstacle to you? If you want to keep a solid relationship with your family, it is most important to manage this process with respect. Think about finding ways to create common ground among you. When there are a lot of differences, apply the following:

Guidelines for Handling Differences

Explore and understand the difference. Use questions like:

- How do you see this? Why?
- What are the benefits of your point of view?
- How do you believe I see it?
- What are the benefits of my point of view?

Figure out what your common ground is. Use questions like:

- What do we agree on? What do we see the same way?
- What things do we all value? What's important to us?
- What are the things that you don't want to do without?
- What does everybody need through this process to feel heard and respected?

View this as a future to create, not a problem to solve.

- What else is possible?
- What could this future, or that one, look like?
- How might we get from here to there?

Look at disagreements as information, not as more stuff to get hot and upset about. Listen to all the voices in your family, and dig for the foundation of agreement that exists. Focus your effort on joint development of the future. That way there is no one right answer. You want this to be a co-creative process, where all input is valued, but not towards any predetermined outcome.

Whatever common ground you share — no matter how basic or simple — it provides the cornerstone for sustaining your relationship. Here is a heads-up on two typical conversations during these times of transition.

Tips for Handling the Expected Questions

Security and safety. Be prepared to find your common ground on issues like:

- Can you earn enough money to feed and house yourself?
- To take care of emergencies?
- To have adequate health care?

Happiness and using your potential. Find your common ground on questions like:

- What will make you happy?
- How will you use your talents?
- Will you be with people who care about you?
- Will you be someplace you can grow and learn?

These are the places to start. Look for agreements and situations where your thinking overlaps, and this will give you enough take-off space to launch your own thing.

What to Do When You Can't Get Through

These how-tos for managing parents are focused on families that are pretty stable. None are perfectly stable all the time — but I'm talking about the usual ups and downs of family life. If you suspect your family is under extra stress, this section is for you.

Families are peculiar little social groups — you can feel like they tie you down, yet feel lost without the anchor they provide. Sometimes, no matter how hard you try, you can't get your parents or your support group to work collaboratively with you. There may even be situations where you have to step pretty far away and risk those relationships in order to fulfill your potential. Sometimes families can even be destructive or toxic to one another.

If you are wondering about whether this may be true for you, I advise you to get some professional counseling to sort things out. This stuff isn't easy, but at the same time I don't want you to label your situation with the skull and crossbones just yet — because you could be over-reacting. Our emotions in times like these can be pretty unreliable. So get the help you need to wade through this — sometimes that is professional counseling, and sometimes it means getting a reality check from friends and mentors.

Whatever decision you make, whether it be to stay and work things out, or to pave your own way alone, continue to apply the tips we have talked about here — be honest, open, respectful and considerate. Do your part to build whatever bridges are open to you, then chart your own path and look for support in other places. Leave a door open for a future time when everyone may be more ready to band together in support of one another.

Preparing Your Launch Pad

If you think about it, the best compliment to parents is when their children strike out on their own. It means they have prepared them well — with skills of confidence, responsibility, adventure and the practicalities of survival. But the bittersweet sensation of stepping onto the launch pad often colors our perception — all of us, child and family — of what an exciting time this is. Our fears creep in, especially of the unknown.

Remember what you know about easing the transition. Sometimes it pays off to be there for your parents, to be 100 percent on and listening to their needs and wants. There have been many times in the past — whether it was taking care of you when you were sick, or giving up a whole weekend to help you move out of an apartment — that they were 100 percent on for you.

That's the beauty of supportive family relationships — there is a willingness to be 100 percent giving for the other person, and to trade off that role. And just like you've gotten some tips here to smooth the transition, parents can benefit from similar tips, slanted towards their perspective on all of this. You can point them in that direction by sending them to the Web at www.ChooseOnPurpose.com — a parents section is there to help.

So part of stepping onto the launch pad is spending the time to ensure that all your support systems are in place. Spend some time with those parents, reassure them that you have all your gear, you've trained well, and they've done their job well. You're ready.

For most of us, our support team wants to help. We all just need a few tools and techniques — like the questions and conversation starters above — for getting to the launch pad and finding our new role. It's time for parents to step back and become coaches and cheerleaders. And it's time for you to simply step up.

Make a few notes below for yourself on what you want to concentrate on as you begin to manage your parents more strategically, strengthening the bonds of a lifetime.

 Strategy: Strengthen Bonds with Your Parents

1. Reflect on what both you and your parents need.

- What kind of reassurance do your parents need right now?
- How can you best keep them informed and reassured?
- What can you tell them about your needs?
- What will help you stay calm when tensions rise?

2. Create a plan.

- Identify activities you can invest time in that will help smooth the way in this transition. (For example, setting aside nights for dinner together, keeping up your recreational activities together — such as going to a baseball game, walking together, shopping together, etc.)
- Identify ways to remind yourself to keep your parents informed and engaged. (For example, don't let another Sunday slip by without remembering to catch them up on your week's work.)
- Identify ways to encourage them to let you go. (For example, what responsibilities can you take on, what boundaries can you set?)

Parents and family are a significant part of your launch pad. Use them, rely on them, manage them, love them, and don't forget to thank them for being there for you.

Power up Your Elevator Pitch

What You'll Find

This section helps you take your stand in this world. What are you all about? What do you have to offer? You will get help writing a clear declaration of what you contribute to the world and staying on your game.

Help with Your Elevator Pitch

Your Declaration Statement, and ultimately your Elevator Pitch, works because it pulls you into the present moment and literally makes a statement about how you are powerful in the world. Marianne Williamson's words in *A Return to Love: Reflections on the Principles of "A Course in Miracles"* fit here:

> "Our deepest fear is not that we are inadequate. Our deepest fear is that we are powerful beyond measure. It is our light, not our darkness that most frightens us. We ask ourselves, Who am I to be brilliant, gorgeous, talented, fabulous? Actually, who are you not to be? You are a child of God. Your playing small does not serve the world. There is nothing enlightened about shrinking so that other people won't feel insecure around you. We are all meant to shine, as children do. We were born to make manifest the glory of God that is within us. It's not just in some of us; it's in everyone. And as we let our own light shine, we unconsciously give other people permission to do the same. As we are liberated from our own fear, our presence automatically liberates others."

The only way you can do that is by taking a stand. Do this by declaring with strong verbs, adjectives and adverbs what role you will play in the world.

Below you will find two lists, one with verbs, the other with adjectives. Review it to help you find active, powerful descriptors to help you write a great statement.

Verbs That Describe Your Skills and Contribution

Achieve	*Express*	*Persevere*	*Serve*
Administer	*Extract*	*Persuade*	*Service*
Analyze	*Figure*	*Photograph*	*Set*
Assemble	*File*	*Pilot*	*Sew*
Build	*Finance*	*Plan*	*Shape*
Calculate	*Imagine*	*Problem solve*	*Speak*
Communicate	*Implement*	*Produce*	*Study*
Compose	*Improve*	*Promote*	*Summarize*
Consult	*Improvise*	*Publicize*	*Supervise*
Control	*Increase*	*Purchase*	*Supply*
Coordinate	*Influence*	*Question*	*Take instruction*
Copy	*Interview*	*Raise*	*Talk*
Count	*Invent*	*Read*	*Teach/train*
Create	*Judge*	*Realize*	*Tell*
Debate	*Keep*	*Reason*	*Troubleshoot*
Define	*Lead*	*Receive*	*Tutor*
Deliver	*Lecture*	*Recommend*	*Type*
Draw	*Listen*	*Reconcile*	*Umpire*
Edit	*Maintain*	*Record*	*Understand*
Elicit	*Make*	*Recruit*	*Unify*
Eliminate	*Manage*	*Reduce*	*Upgrade*
Emphasize	*Manipulate*	*Refer*	*Use*
Enforce	*Motivate*	*Remember*	*Utilize*
Establish	*Negotiate*	*Repair*	*Verbalize*
Estimate	*Observe*	*Research*	*Weigh*
Evaluate	*Organize*	*Schedule*	*Work*
Examine	*Originate*	*Select*	*Write*
Expand	*Paint*	*Sell*	
Experiment	*Perceive*	*Sense*	
Explain	*Perform*	*Separate*	

Adjectives That Describe Your Personal Traits

Adaptive	*Disciplined*	*Innovative*	*Positive*
Adaptable	*Discreet*	*Instrumental*	*Precise*
Adept	*Efficient*	*Interpersonal*	*Productive*
Broad-minded	*Energetic*	*Logical*	*Realistic*
Collaborative	*Enterprising*	*Loyal*	*Reliable*
Competent	*Experienced*	*Mature*	*Resourceful*
Conscientious	*Fair*	*Methodical*	*Self-reliant*
Creative	*Firm*	*Objective*	*Sensitive*
Dependable	*Forceful*	*Outgoing*	*Sincere*
Detailed	*Funny;*	*Participative*	*Successful*
Determined	*light-hearted*	*Personable*	*Tactful*
Diplomatic	*Honest*	*Pleasant*	*Versatile*

These lists are not meant to be exhaustive, but to get you started on thinking about precise and powerful ways to describe your contribution to the world. Use the thesaurus to get exactly the right word if you don't find it here. These great words will come in handy for many needs — from resume to interviews.

Your declaration uses the words like this:

I   **[strong verb, present tense]**
       [your target/goal]
       [adjectives/adverbs]

It looks like this:

I   create
       graphic designs that
       express a dramatic story in a single image.

Examples of Great Declarations

They always tell a story and let people know the stand you take in the world. Here are a few, including my own.

"I facilitate great learning experiences by being grounded, objective, light-hearted and focused."

"I edit books with clarity, precision and grace."

"I deliver health care consulting services with tact, knowledge, humor and a collaborative approach."

 Strategy: Practice for Your Declaration/Elevator Pitch

Think about:

Using the best verbs, adjectives and adverbs to describe the goals of your Declaration and ultimately your Elevator Pitch.

Write Your Declaration

I **[strong verb, present tense]**

   [your target/goal]

   [adjectives/adverbs]

This is the guts of your elevator pitch.

Where You Can Use Your Elevator Pitch

Your resume, cover letters, thank you notes and interviews can all reiterate parts of your pitch. With your statement, you have a home base to go back to when you are communicating with people. The more consistent you are, the louder people will hear your message and what you can deliver. Using my own declaration statement on facilitation, here is an example of where I have included it in my own information and networking process:

Resume: "Facilitation skills" listed in skill section at top

Cover letter/Proposal: mentions "my ability to ground participants in what is important, while focusing them on achieving results they can be proud of."

Thank you note: "I think we have zeroed in on the right targets for change. By combining my facilitation skills with your focus, we'll make some good stuff happen for the team!"

Don't forget, this is your message to the world, so keep repeating it with consistent words wherever you are.

Unsticking Stuckness

What You'll Find

Definition of Stuck and How We Get Stuck

We humans are masters at getting stuck. What we're not so smart about sometimes, though, is recognizing when we're stuck and then figuring out how to get out of it.

There's a story that used to circulate in corporate training classes about how to adapt to change. It's about a frog that gets stuck in a big pot of water. At room temperature, everything is fine. But if someone turns on the heat, the change happens so slowly that the frog doesn't even notice the water is boiling until it's too late to do anything. So paying attention to what's happening around you is really the key to surviving and thriving.

The definition of stuck is

> to be fixed in a particular position,
> unable to move or be moved.

How do you know if you're stuck?

- Other people tell you so (they see you sweating)
- You complain about the same thing all the time
- You resist your current situation with anger/resentment

What do these look like in real life?

- A friend sits you down and tells you what it's like seeing the same destructive behavior from you day after day.
- You complain about your job (again) but you and the person you complain to know you aren't moving an inch.
- You come home every day from work annoyed and grouchy because the situation grates on you and leaves you listless.

Like the frog, it's hard not only to be aware of being stuck, but too often we give up before we even consider changing — often because we've spent so much energy resisting and complaining, we have little left for the change. It's time to divert that stream of energy to getting unstuck.

Are You on the "Stuck List"? and How to Get Off

Getting unstuck is as simple as deciding to unstick yourself. But as I've said before, simple is not necessarily easy to do. It requires you not only to make a decision, but to do something about it to "unfix" yourself from a particular position and to *move*.

Work though this checklist below. If you're caught in a loop on any one of the following feelings, then face it—you're stuck.

Strategy: Consult the Stuck List

Check one or more that apply.

___ I'm not appreciated for what I can do
___ I don't like what I'm doing
___ I can't make a difference
___ They don't like how I work
___ I feel like no one wants me
___ This is too frustrating
___ I don't believe enough in myself
___ There's nothing out there that I will like
___ I won't be able to pay the bills
___ My family will kill me if I do that
___ I'm not having any fun
___ I don't have enough money to make the change
___ I'm afraid to leave what I have now
___ It might not work out
___ It's a big risk
___ I'll have to start over and that's too much to ask
___ I've never done this before
___ They won't let me be creative
___ They keep getting in my way
___ This is a dead-end situation
___ I don't have anyone to talk to
___ No one likes the way I do it
___ It's too much work
___ It will cause a fight if I try to do what I want to do
___ What if I fail?
___ Other_____

Now that you're not in denial anymore, see suggestions below to get comfortable with the confusion and create a way out.

Everybody gets stuck! This is why we need others around us to help. Often, we cannot see that we are stuck. We convince ourselves that it is "circumstances," or the fault of "others" that got us into this situation. And that's when we lose the ability to be *response – ABLE*. Stuck implies inability to move. So here are three principles of getting unstuck.

1. Deal with the denial
2. Get comfortable with the confusion
3. Create a way out

First, Deal with Denial. We humans can't stand admitting we're stuck. We think it makes us look weak and ineffective. The fact is, it makes us human.

If any of the items on the *Stuck List* strike a chord, then this shaping your life thing has you stuck. At some point, if you can pull your head up, something or someone will help you shake off the denial that you are stuck. Then you can do something about it.

This is where our old 3Fs tricks come in to play — fighting, freezing, or fleeing. I suggest you revisit pages 143–150 in Chapter 7: *Managing Yourself* to put the tips to work that will help kick you out of denial.

That's dealing with denial. It's as simple as standing up, becoming ABLE to respond to the situation, and admitting you are stuck. Then you can move on to dealing with the confusion.

Second, Get Comfortable with the Confusion. This is the part where you get on your horse and ride willingly into the dark forest. You're going to get lost, you're going to stumble, and you may even have to kill a dragon or two while you're in there (your own fears, that is). But it's part of the adventure, so saddle up.

The best way to deal with confusion is to build a bridge from "there and then" (your stuckness and denial) to the "here and now" — your ability to respond to your situation and shape your life the way you want to. It's really hard to get up one day and announce to yourself that you have changed.

While you can utter the words, the guts of the change, as you know, comes in what you do. You've probably heard the old adage: Insanity is doing the same thing and expecting different results. Well, if all you do is tell yourself you've changed your mind, but keep doing the same things — you're still stuck in the same old insanity.

So rather than working on changing your mind, work on changing the feelings you have — the way your body responds to the stuckness you are feeling. If you feel stressed, tired, agitated — work on changing that first. This means getting your body and your heart in the game. You may need to relax more, laugh more, get a hobby, get more exercise, and get some space to focus on becoming aware of when you get agitated. Basically, get your mind out of the way. Stop thinking so much.

Once you have your feelings working for you, your ability to see what to do next can come more easily — as a by-product of feeling better, rather than the goal. Think about what happens when you try to learn something new — whether it's basket weaving, playing a sport, or playing the piano. If you're stuck on learning the move, like, say a golf swing — your over-focus usually ends up in tightening and hardening your muscles. The tighter you are, the harder it is to slide into the new practice.

Once you're loose, it becomes easier to cope with the confusion of the new habits you are building. You build some muscle memory and your feelings and muscles just take over for you. Now, it becomes easier to start skating across that bridge from there and then to here and now.

Third, Create a Way Out. Once you've accepted the confusion and have started working on loosening yourself up, it's time to get dirty and work in the Stuck Muck. While you may be ready to set a goal, be prepared to flop around for a while, as if you were a kid in a mud puddle — slipping and sliding as you try to get a grip and pull yourself out.

In order to create a way out, you must be willing to focus on what you want, and practice it — including dealing with the slips and falls, getting right into the messiness of the transition — jumping into the muck. Then practice until you see improvement — sometimes in leaps, sometimes in small steps, and finally getting to the point where you're doing the new stuff. It looks like this, stepping down into the muck, then working your way up to accomplishing your goal. It's messy, but it works.

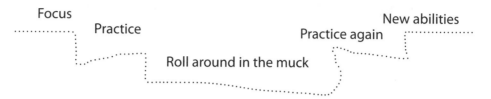

Focus
Practice
Roll around in the muck
Practice again
New abilities

Here are two examples in my own life. The first is about writing this book. It took an enormous amount of focus and goal setting to switch out of my full-time consulting role — traveling all the time, busy, in demand, and into a role where I often felt like a hermit — spending days on end working in my at-home office, hardly venturing out as I leaned over my keyboard for hours on end.

It takes a lot of practice to write, get kicked in the gut with edits and feedback, and get back to writing again, only to get rolled over with more "critical" feedback. That's where rolling around in the muck comes in. I spent considerable time on my own self-talk, working my way out of self-flagellating talk: "Am I nuts? I had a good thing going. I'm a lousy writer. I'll never get the hang of this."

But I kept at it, and one day I had a breakthrough. After another feedback round that had me feeling like I'd never find my voice, I sat down one night and banged out twelve pages, using ideas I had been working on, but changing the voice I was using. I printed it out and handed it to my daughter and my husband and asked (well, demanded actually) they read it on the spot. A miracle happened — they both liked it, and I'd finally pierced the bubble — I found my voice.

And what did I do? I kept practicing — kept working on it, and as I did, I saw the new abilities emerging. I used running, yoga, ballroom dancing, and rest as my routes for getting from there and then to here and now. The running energized me, the yoga settled me down, the ballroom dancing reminded me that sometimes it's one step forward, and two steps back, and the rest helped with all the rewiring my brain and heart were doing.

As a result of all this, the writing voice became easier and easier to hear. It took a couple of years, a lot of patience — and a lot of tearing my hair out—but it happened. The best part is I slowly started learning how to have a sense of humor about this and to reduce, even if it was teaspoonful-by-teaspoonful, my self-flagellation. I replaced it with a little more laughter and a lot more patience.

The second example is one I'm still working on — doing a handstand in yoga class. I have more fears wrapped around this one — from I'm not strong enough, to my left hip is whacked out so I can't be steady — to I'm just not the type who can do handstands.

But I have a focus and a determination. Somewhere deep inside of me I believe I can get there. For me it's slow, and step-by-step — practice, practice, practice — while I face my fears of flipping upside down. So I'm still rolling around in the muck on this one, but I'm diligently practicing. I will get there — and I hope if we ever meet, by the time that happens, I will be able to report that I do handstands on a regular basis every week!

Bibliography

Arnett, Jeffrey. *Emerging Adulthood*. New York: Oxford Univerity Press, 2004.

Curlee, Pamela, and Svetlana Masgutova, Ph.D. *Trauma Recovery—You Are a Winner: A New Choice Through Natural Developmental Movements*. Fairfield, IA: 1st World Publishing, 2007.

Doidge, Norman, M.D. *The Brain that Changes Itself*. New York: Penguin Books, 2007.

Florida, Richard. *Who's Your City*. New York: Basic Books, 2008.

Friedman, Thomas L. *The World is Flat*. New York: Farrar, Straus, and Giroux, 2005.

Gilbert, Daniel, Ph.D. *Stumbling on Happiness*. New York: Knopf, 2006.

Hannaford, Carla. *Smart Moves: Why Learning is Not All in Your Head*, 2nd ed. Arlington, VA: Great Ocean Publishers, 2005.

Jobs, Steve. 2005 Commencement Speech, Stanford University.

Herrmann, Ned. *The Creative Brain*. Lake Lure, NC: Brain Books, 1990.

Kabat-Zinn, Jon. *Wherever You Go There You Are*. New York: Hyperion, 1994.

Mlodinow, Leonard. *The Drunkard's Walk: How Randomness Rules Our Lives*. New York: Pantheon Books, 2008.

Osbon, Diane, ed. *Reflections on the Art of Living: A Joseph Campbell Companion*. New York: Harper Perennial, 1991.

Oshry, Barry. *Seeing Systems*, 2nd ed. San Francisco: Berrett-Koehler Publishers, 2007.

Rogers, Fred. *Life's Journeys According to Mister Rogers*. New York: Hyperion, 2005.

Weisbord, Marvin and Sandra Janoff. *Don't Just Do Something, Stand There!* San Francisco: Berret-Koehler Publishers, 2007.

Williamson, Marianne. *A Return to Love: Reflections on the Principles of "A Course in Miracles."* New York: HarperCollins, 1992.

Index

Meet Susan Berg, PhD

Call her a transition expert. An award-winning international speaker, facilitator, and now author of *Choose on Purpose for Twentysomethings*, Susan Berg brings real world experience and solutions to the issues facing young people today. Her career-long focus on mastering change has won praise from Fortune 500 giants and renowned humanitarian non-profits alike. This same ability now helps to guide twentysomethings through the minefield of early adulthood.

Berg earned her Ph.D. in Adult Education and Development from the University of California, Los Angeles, her M.A. from Northwestern University, and B.A. Cum Laude from Miami University in Ohio. Initially an educator and school administrator in California and Texas, she honed her focus on designing strategic change projects. Those skills transferred perfectly to her more than ten years at Unisys Corporation, where she was awarded the prestigious Chairman's Innovation Award for implementing new teamwork practices for the tasks of the 21st century.

Today, Susan Berg is Managing Partner and Founder of Compass Associates, a results-based consulting firm specializing in making projects happen in the face of disputes, "un-clarity," and confusion.

Not surprisingly, Susan is also the mother of two thriving twentysomethings. This experience, coupled with her know-how in change management, drives her passion for working with twentysomethings, and indeed anyone who is willing to be a beginner and make bold moves.

Susan shares her home in Doylestown, Pennsylvania, with her beloved husband, her feisty ninetysomething mother, two dogs and a cat—with a swinging door for the comings and goings of her twentysomething kids and their friends.

Contact Susan directly at susan.berg@ChooseOnPurpose.com
Find more resources at www.ChooseOnPurpose.com

Group for
Purposeful
Solutions

GPS

About the Advisory Network

Choose on Purpose for Twentysomethings has flourished under the guidance of its advisory network — the GPS. Our remarkable team, with its unique GPS approach — known as the Group for Purposeful Solutions — has supported the development of *Choose on Purpose* in every way imaginable.

This dedicated crew helped cultivate my idea and provided much feedback along the way. They road tested it as readers, critics, and "coachees." And they were there to celebrate at its publication. The team includes all kinds of people — from twentysomethings to fiftysomethings, career searchers to career builders, millennials to boomers, kids and parents, the shy and the assertive, the artistic and the analytical.

We share its success together and encourage you to dive in and let this current carry you as well. My deepest thanks to the GPS pioneers: Abby, Andrew, Janis, Jim, Kate, Kirstin, Kristen, Mary, Matt, Rachael and Sean. Read their stories at www.ChooseOnPurpose.com — where we help each other bring our talent to life.